THE ULTIMATE GUIDE TO HIKING

THE ULTIMATE GUIDE TO HIKING

MORE THAN 100 ESSENTIAL SKILLS ON CAMPSITES, GEAR, WILDLIFE, MAP READING, AND MORE

LEN McDOUGALL

Skyhorse Publishing

Skyhorse Publishing books may be purchased in bulk at special discounts for sales promotion, corporate gifts, fund-raising, or educational purposes. Special editions can also be created to specifications. For details, contact the Special Sales Department, Skyhorse Publishing, 307 West 36th Street, 11th Floor, New York, NY 10018 or info@skyhorsepublishing.com.

Skyhorse® and Skyhorse Publishing® are registered trademarks of Skyhorse Publishing, Inc.®, a Delaware corporation.

Visit our website at www.skyhorsepublishing.com.

10 9 8 7 6 5 4 3 2 1

Library of Congress Cataloging-in-Publication Data is available on file.

Cover design by Brian Peterson
Cover photo credit: iStock

Print ISBN: 978-1-5107-4276-5
Ebook ISBN: 978-1-5107-4280-2

Printed in China

TABLE OF CONTENTS

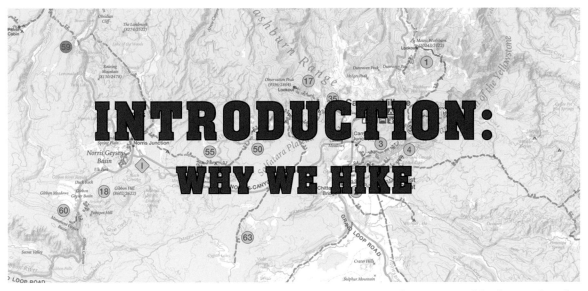

INTRODUCTION:
WHY WE HIKE

Why do we hike? What is it that possesses us to venture on foot into wild places that by their very nature lack the conveniences, services, and luxuries that twenty-first-century people have come to take for granted? Why would anyone enter into an environment that may be so removed from civilization that cellular telephones can't get a signal? Such places can, and sometimes have, claimed the lives of unprepared. Some locations are so remote that outside help, at your best speed, might be more than half a day away.

The answer to the question of why we voluntarily brave such hardships and potential danger is, in a single word, adventure. Most of us have the desire to explore that drove early Americans to carve homes from wilderness, to clear and plant the land for farms that would sustain future generations of pioneers. From the base provided by these first homesteaders there sprang a small army of rovers and voyagers who fulfilled President Thomas Jefferson's vision of linking the United States of America from sea to shining sea.

As a hiker, you're following in the footsteps of heroes like Captain Meriwether Lewis and Second Lieutenant William Clark, whose expedition across unknown territory, using only the most basic of navigational tools,

We have a long tradition of venturing far and wide into places where the faint of heart will not be found.

With the finest wilderness trekking gear ever invented, and a little guidance from those who went before them, the hikers of today are fully capable of visiting (and helping to protect) our world's vanishing wilderness places.

proved that the West Coast of the United States bordered the Pacific Ocean. Because of those first footsteps of Lewis and Clark, and those who created the Oregon Trail after them, you can tread the same paths with almost none of the rigors and dangers that they faced.

Perhaps most importantly, because of those early explorers, you can have a detailed map. Modern maps present an aerial picture of the mountains, rivers, and other terrain features that came as a surprise to early explorers. You can know what you're getting into before you get into it.

Even so, don't for an instant think that trekking into a wilderness area is not an adventure. Ask the oldest, most learned outdoors person, and they'll tell you that virtually every outing reveals something they'd never seen before. The study of nature, a prime motivation for hikers in any environment, can blossom into a lifelong educational endeavor. If you spent every day out of doors with a tablet computer, or even just pencil and notebook, you couldn't see or record every nuance that normally occurs in the natural world in a very long lifetime.

And that is why we hike: to see sights, to smell fragrances, to experience feelings not available anywhere except in forests, deserts, and mountains that are far from the bustle of human civilizations. We hike because we are afflicted with the same desire to see what lies over the next rise, a desire that spurred the earliest American frontiersmen and their families to carve a primordial continent into the greatest nation in the history of the world.

But remember, a smart hiker never hikes alone. Always take a

The children of our pioneer forebears were taught to safely handle every aspect of their lives, from fire to firearms, and today's hikers can experience at least a taste of that frontier life.

buddy along. It's more fun that way, and it's a whole lot safer for both of you.

See you on the trail.

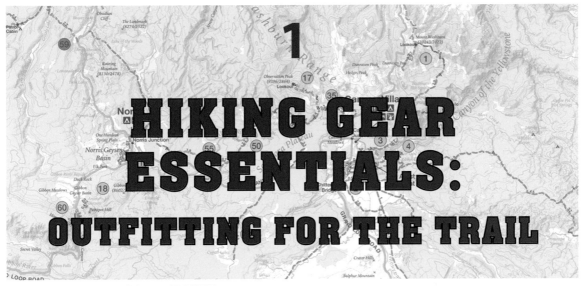

HIKING GEAR ESSENTIALS: OUTFITTING FOR THE TRAIL

THE WELL-DRESSED HIKER

Popular culture has promoted a naked-into-the-wilderness myth in recent years, but the truth is that Native Americans, Aborigines, and frontiersmen did not venture into wilderness without having as much equipment for safety and comfort as they could carry. Early people lived in wilderness, and they were only too aware, personally and vicariously, of how a single misstep could cost even the most skilled their lives. There was no 9-1-1, no telephones, sometimes no nearby neighbors, and often no one to rely on except themselves.

Perhaps ironically, the most capable, yet least experienced, wilderness trekkers are living today, in an age of plastics, microconductor electronics, and ultralight materials. Today's hikers have access to tools that our forefathers and foremothers could only have dreamed of if they possessed vivid imaginations. Ponder for a moment how valuable the ordinary resealable plastic containers that we throw away by the millions every single day (and which often end up in the oceans and forests) would have been to people for whom sealed containers were limited to cork-sealed glass, horn, and sewn rawhide. It has been said that if a person were thrown back in time three hundred years

Indigenous people or pioneers on any continent didn't trek into wilderness without taking as many potentially life-saving tools as were possible to carry, not the least of which was protective clothing.

Many of the plastic containers, wire ties, and other items that we toss out as trash every day would have had lifesaving value to the frontier folk who forged civilizations from wilderness.

and could only take one thing, a good choice would be a filled dumpster, whose contents would make them wildly wealthy.

That same philosophy applies to everything about wilderness exploration—especially clothing. The garments of today offer better comfort, warmth, and utility than in any generation before, and it behooves every hiker to employ those advantages in their own hiking outfits.

One bit of advice that every hiker should heed, as it has proven immensely valuable over the decades, is to button or otherwise close pockets after replacing whatever item they carry. The importance of securing pockets that have that option cannot be overstated.

TRAIL-WORTHY FOOTWEAR

Once, while backpacking a section of the North Country Trail in Mackinac State Forest, I stopped at an overgrown bank along the Carp River to refill my canteen. As I knelt at the water's edge, pumping my water filter's handle, my eyes played over the streambank, taking in tracks from the many animals that visited there daily.

Then I saw them: a pair of hiking boots sitting neatly together on the sand under the shadow of an overhanging river willow. Closer inspection revealed the boots, now partially obscured by rough sawgrasses and sand, had been there for about a year. Leather and vinyl were cracked from repeated exposure to rain, snow, and sun, but the boots were otherwise sound, and appeared to have been in good shape when they were abandoned.

Based on clues at the scene, it appeared those boots had been purposely left behind by a hiker who just couldn't bear to wear them another mile. They bore mute testimony to the fact that trekking in a poorly fitting pair of boots can be harder on one's feet than going barefoot.

Hikers, by definition, are people who spend a lot of time walking over uneven terrain that can range from flat to downright tortuous. Most are bearing more than their own body weight, from the ten pounds or so of gear carried by day hikers to the fifty-pound backpacks of wilderness adventurers who won't be returning home before next week. These and other folks who traverse long stretches of backcountry afoot need all the comfort, support, and armor their boots can provide.

Good boots are essential to determining whether an outing is spent appreciating the innumerable wonders of nature or in preoccupation with the misery of blisters and aching feet, and hikers of all disciplines need to regard footwear with a critical eye. The differences between a hiking boot that will earn your affection and one that you'll be tempted to leave behind aren't always apparent. Walk into a typical shoe store, and you're likely to be overwhelmed by an array of outdoor footwear that ranges from completely inadequate to outstanding.

Price and quality don't always indicate how well a boot will perform. A top-flight mountaineering boot designed to use crampons and to kick toe holds in vertical ice walls might look handsome and carry a hefty price tag, but a mountaineering boot is necessarily hard soled, and too inflexible to permit the freedom of movement a hiker's foot needs. Regardless of quality, it's simply the wrong

This abandoned pair of hiking boots bears mute testimony to the fact that a poor pair of boots is worse than going barefoot.

boot for hiking, and those who try it will regret the effort. Most boots carry a tag stating the purpose for which they're intended, and it's best to focus on models made for the activity you have in mind. Hiking boots are for hiking with a light backpack, while more supportive, more sturdily built backpacking boots are for loads of one-third your own body weight or more.

Name brands should be given the most consideration. There's nothing commercial in that statement, only a recognition that reputable boot makers have an image to uphold, like Mercedes-Benz cars or Apple computers, and their products are held to higher standards. That, combined with sometimes fierce competition between recognized labels, can net some very good deals for consumers. Names to look for include Asolo, Vasque, La Sportiva, Raichle, and Danner.

Competition between manufacturers also means that boot designs are continually changing. The frustrating side of this never-ending evolution is that a boot you really like will often be revamped or phased out within a year of its introduction. The upside is that shoppers on a budget can find good bargains among still new but discontinued models on internet sites such as Amazon and eBay.

One trend that the ladies among us can benefit from is a growing number of women's boots that are engineered to accommodate the slighter build of the female foot. According to marketing managers at Lowa and Danner, there has been a notable increase in the number of women who participate in outdoors activities like hunting, backpacking, and birdwatching. The result has been a corresponding increase in demand for women's footwear that has made it profitable for boot makers to introduce new lines created specifically for women.

Light hiking boots like these are suitable for carrying a twenty-pound daypack and represent the ongoing commitment toward the creation of perfect footwear.

No longer do ladies have to settle for the best fit they can find in a men's boot.

Once you've narrowed a boot store's wares down to the most suitable candidates, there are a number of features that every good outdoors boot should have. The farther a boot's lacing extends down the instep toward the toe, the better it can be custom fitted to the unique contours of its wearer's foot. Beginning at the ankle joint, laces should cross the instep no less than four times. Avoid low-top "trail" hikers that don't extend upward far enough to encase the ankle joint. High-top boots are made to surround and support the ankle above and below its joint, making it more difficult to accidentally twist or pull ligaments beyond their limits.

Boot soles should be deeply lugged and aggressive, the kind on shoes that must be removed at the door when you get home, lest they track-in clumps of mud. Real-life woodsmen know, or soon learn the hard way, that smooth-soled footwear virtually guarantees their wearer's buttocks will make frequent jarring contact with the earth. (There was once a fellow who no one would hunt with because he insisted on wearing basketball-type shoes, and he frequently landed hard on his wallet with a shotgun in his hands. Safety is important.) Whether in the form of claws, rough pads, or sharp-edged hooves, every animal that walks or flies possesses some type of traction to provide a sure grip on slippery surfaces, and bipedal humans need that advantage more than most.

Unless you can fly, protection from cold, moisture, and injuries is an imperative for every hiker of any stripe.

Many better hiking and hunting boots incorporate a microfabric bootie (e.g., Gore-Tex) sandwiched between their liners and shells. This doesn't actually make the boot waterproof—the flexing action of walking through water will eventually force moisture through the membrane—but it will keep water out while wading shallow, narrow streams or walking through dew-wet grass. In wet conditions, a microfabric bootie will keep your feet a lot drier than a boot that doesn't have that feature, and its breathability permits moisture to evaporate more quickly.

THE WOODSMAN'S TIE

A woodsman's tie, as it has been historically known, is a way to substantially increase the ankle support of any ankle-high, lace-up boot. This simple method of tying boots greatly decreases chances that a hiker's foot will slip off a wet log or roll sideways on a loose stone and force an ankle joint beyond its limits.

Considering its value to a hiker, the woodsman's tie is simple enough to be tied by anyone who can tie their own shoes. Just tie your hiking boots as you would normally. When you reach their tops, where you would normally tie them into a bow, cross the laces and wrap them snugly around the back, bringing their ends back around to the front. Many boot makers provide extra-long laces to enable this ankle-wrap. Finally, secure the wrapped laces with a square knot. You will be left with no bow loops to snag on brush and pull untied, just loose ends that won't catch against anything. Or, if you prefer, those lace ends can be further concealed by pushing them between a boot's tongue and ankle collar.

An example of a woodsman's tie on a hiking boot.

Your companions might gasp a little when they see you tie your laces into a knot, but as many hikers know, a square knot is both secure and easy to untie. Just pull the top, outermost loop made by the knot, and it will come loose. From personal experience, boot laces tied into a square knot are easy to untie even when caked with ice.

Whenever possible, try on boots before you purchase them, because an unsuitable pair cannot be returned after you've walked just a few miles in them. Wear the same socks you'll wear hiking, and tie the boots completely—many blisters are self-inflicted because some hikers refuse to lace and tie their footwear properly. The fit should be snug but comfortable, with plenty of room in the toe box (scrunched-together toes cause bunions), and you should feel slight upward pressure against your arches. When you walk across the floor there should be a sensation of rolling forward as weight transfers from heel to toe, as though the soles were spring loaded. Ideally, there should be no pinch points or rub spots, because areas of slight discomfort in the store can become downright painful on the trail.

The old and the new; hikers tend to hang on to old boots even after they've worn out, because an older boot is creased, bent, and otherwise conditioned to mate precisely with its wearer's foot and the way they walk.

After you've purchased the boots you like, wear them at least ten miles in a safe environment close to home. Breaking in new boots isn't nearly the contest between skin and leather that it used to be, but new, unbroken boots still need to be creased or stretched in the right places to accommodate an individual's unique walking style. Once broken in, your boots will be custom-fitted to your feet, but taking stiff new boots into an environment where you might need to hike many miles a day can make you dislike even the good ones before they've had a fair chance.

Expect to pay at least one hundred dollars for a good pair of boots. That might seem exorbitant when compared to less expensive but similar looking models in discount stores, but the best qualities in a boot made for hard outdoor use are often concealed within its construction. In the long run, paying more for a premium boot makes better financial sense, because it will probably hold up better (usually much better) than discount store brands, and you may not have to replace them for many years. But the real dividend is comfort; it's tough to be in a good mood or to appreciate the beauty of your surroundings when your feet are killing you. Be kind to your feet and dress them as well as you can. They'll return the favor many times over.

SOCKS

Socks are a critical component of any outdoor outfit, and even day hikers can do well to have a dry pair stashed in a pocket. In a survival situation, you cannot be too kind to your feet, because they are probably the vehicle that will take you home. Proper socks can also make a big difference in how your feet feel at the end of a long day. Even in summer, experienced long-haul hikers prefer a two-sock system consisting of a thick wool-blend outer sock worn over a light synthetic liner sock.

Cotton in any amount is bad; cotton socks can make feet feel cold in the best boots, while a good sock system gets maximum comfort and warmth from an inadequate boot. Avoid the mistake of pulling on additional socks, as these can constrict circulation through the feet and actually make them cold. With good boots and socks, you can master any terrain or temperature on the planet.

Socks are also a layered system, with a lightweight, slippery liner sock of nonabsorbent material, covered by a thicker insulated outer sock. Outer socks start at about twelve dollars per pair, but most give years of service. The liner sock, which can be any inexpensive department-store nylon or rayon dress-type sock, provides a slippery antifriction barrier to prevent hot spots, while the cushioned outer sock allows boots to be tied snugly but comfortably. Perhaps more importantly, the two nonabsorbent socks work together to wick away moisture, leaving feet feeling much drier, even when boots are wet inside. Liner socks begin at about six dollars a pair at outfitter stores, but department store acrylic dress socks are cheaper, and perform nearly as well in the field.

One of the most over-looked, but important, items of hiking gear is a good pair of socks.

Between liner socks, cushioned outer socks, and well-fitting, properly tied hiking boots, there should ideally be a friction-less environment for a walker's feet. But feet need breaking-in almost as much as footwear, and many occasional hikers often do not have feet that are calloused or toughened in the right areas.

For that reason, self-adhesive moleskin patches (actually made from medical-grade fabric) in various sizes should be part of every hiking outfit. At the first sign of a hot spot—a sore rub-spot that precedes a blister—cover that area directly with the appropriate size moleskin patch. Should a blister form, you must first release the pressure caused by a bubble of fluid by piercing a small hole at a blister's base using a large, sterilized carpet needle or a sharply pointed knife. Express (squeeze out) as much fluid as possible, and cover the deflated blister with moleskin. Should the blister again become a bubble, repeat the piercing procedure and re-cover with moleskin.

Gore-Tex oversocks are an ultralight accessory that have proven their worth since their inception in the 1990s. In personal experiences, these useful oversocks have made sandals into virtually waterproof (and leech-proof) boots in sedimentary ponds, and as overnight camp booties in winter and summer for those middle-of-the-night trips to the pee-tree. Possibly best of all, they add considerable warmth to the aforementioned sock system, without squeezing-off circulation to the feet.

Dry socks are more important than clean underwear **is a time-honored adage that applies to outdoors-lovers of all disciplines, none more than hikers and backpackers.**

TROUSERS

Military-type six-pocket trousers are almost always the order of the day. Large thigh pockets with fasten-down flaps are habit forming. You might not believe how handy a flattened roll of toilet paper carried inside a cargo pocket, sealed inside a ziplock plastic bag will become in the boondocks; in addition to its typical use, you can also use TP for cleaning eyeglass, binocular, and camera lenses.

Cotton or cotton-blend denim blue jeans are not the ideal choice for hiking. They tend to be styled to provide a tight fit, restricting a hiker from getting into the often awkward positions demanded when ducking under a low branch. Ripped-out crotches are almost common.

Additionally, denim material doesn't have the rip-stop weave that has become a standard in trousers designed for working and outdoor activities. A small tear in denim is virtually guaranteed to become a large gash, leaving substantial areas of exposed, unprotected skin. Rip-stop weaves ensure that an accidental tear grows no larger and is much easier to close with needle-and-thread.

Some garment companies are offering BDU (Battle Dress Uniform)–styled work pants made of rip-stop fabrics, but sometimes featuring even more pockets-within-pockets than their GI counterparts and even elastic waistbands. Colors may include khaki or olive drab. Prices start at about eighty dollars per pair.

Bulging thigh pockets attest to the importance that personal storage spaces have to seasoned hikers.

Less expensive trousers and other great buys on trail clothing may be found at resale shops, such as Goodwill. There is a stigma associated with buying clothing (or even daypacks and camping equipment) that has been used by strangers. But except for a rare case of Playground Cooties, there's nothing between those clothes—or a new-looking pair of boots—and you except your own imagination. Even so, I suggest laundering them before wear to at least dampen down that perfume-y scent that resale shops spray on donated fabrics.

Cargo shorts may be permissible in a few places, where biting insects aren't a problem, and you're certain that you won't scrape, scratch, bump, or otherwise inflict injury on your naked calves and knees. In general, it is smarter and more comfortable to cover your legs entirely; wander down by the river into a patch of stinging nettle (*Urtica dioica*), and thousands of acid-tipped hairs show any bared skin why that is true.

UNDERWEAR

Not many normal people like to talk about the clothing layer beneath their outer clothes. It will be discussed here because what you wear next to your skin in cold weather can have genuine impact on how comfortable you'll be. More than a few hikers have been chafed badly enough by their underwear to develop a, sometimes bloody, friction rash that was painful enough to ruin their hike. Do not underestimate the misery that can be caused by the wrong underwear.

Traditional cotton briefs, whether intended for boys or for girls, are not a good choice. Again, cotton is great for bath towels because it absorbs and holds moisture, but that characteristic isn't desirable over a portion of the body that perspires copiously. And because that area is normally kept covered, and thus containing sweat, minimizing moisture there is crucial to keep down odor, chafing, and discomfort while walking.

Most comfortable for hiking and backpacking in warm weather are boxer-type briefs made from a polyester (plastic fiber) material that breathes, absorbs minimal moisture, and slides smoothly over skin. Boxers should be loose fitting, not pinching or binding in any position that one's body can achieve.

To help a good pair of boxers keep you comfortable, every hiker should be equipped with their own cotton-knap washcloth, with a bar of soap contained in a ziplock plastic bag or a personal-size

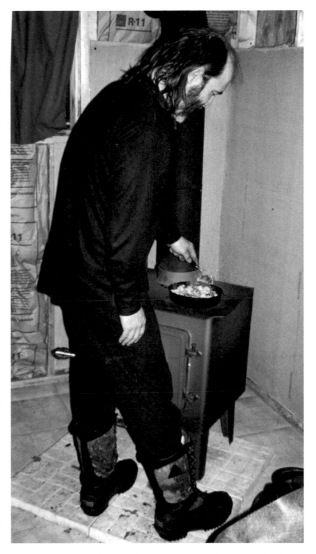

Underwear should always be loose fitting, breathable, and suited to weather conditions. "Long johns," like those in this photo, may be a worthwhile addition to your pack if cold summer rains are possible.

bottle of liquid soap. At the first sign of rubbing or chafing, stop and wash the affected area with a damp cloth and soap (soap removes bacteria in body oils). Wipe off all soap, and apply a little body lotion to the area if you have it.

THE SOAP BAG

Ever since pioneers decided that an occasional bath was conducive to positive social interaction—particularly for hard-working young men in search of wives—and to Divine approval ("Cleanliness is next to God-liness"), people have struggled with the problem of dropping bar soap on the ground. Ground debris like grass, and especially sand, is difficult to remove from wet soap. And a sand-covered bar of soap is like scrubbing your skin with fifty-grit sandpaper. Very uncomfortable, and even damaging to your skin.

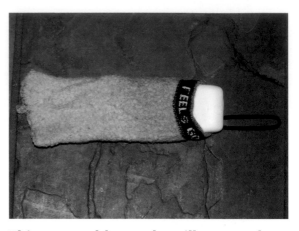

This years-old soap bag illustrates how handy it has been to have a washcloth and soap in a single package. The handy loop sewn to the top means that it can be hung to dry in all but the wettest environments.

Placing wet bar soap in a plastic bag causes it to mold, and drying it in the sun prior to storage makes it a magnet for pine needles, flying insects, and other airborne debris. After several such failed experiments, I hit upon a nearly ideal remedy while boiling coffee with grounds sealed inside a bag made from the ankle portion of a sock (the only part that never wears out), with one end sewn shut, the other tied shut with a shoelace sewn to its open end. This original coffee bag idea yielded wonderful-tasting coffee in any volume required (depending on how much coffee was used), but without the unpleasant grounds of traditional "camp" coffee.

By applying that same sock-bag premise to a bar of soap, which fits quite nicely into the sock bag, you combine soap and washcloth in a single package that will continue to lather until the soap inside is entirely used up. Soap tends not to fall out, even if you leave the top open or if the soap piece is very small. Best of all, if you drop a soap bag on the ground and it becomes covered with sand and pine needles, a quick rinse in water makes the fabric clean again.

So don't just throw the ankle portion of worn-out socks into the trash. Soap bags last practically forever, and they can help use those small pieces of soap that are normally thrown out. You might even decide that you need a soap bag in your shower at home—I did.

Do not share your wash cloth or bar soap with others. Doing so almost ensures that whatever fungal or bacterial infection (usually in the form of a rash, initially) that you might contract will be passed along to the borrower and vice versa. If you must share a washcloth, immersing it entirely in boiling water for a minute kills parasitic, fungal, viral, and bacterial organisms that might be within its fibers.

Other items that go hand-in-hand with this topic are a tube of antifungal cream in a hiker's first-aid kit (always have a first-aid kit), perhaps with a small bottle of medicated powder. If you develop a rash, or even a serious itch that won't stop, wash the area as soon as possible, and apply a light layer of antifungal cream. If you cannot wash, rub medicated powder onto the itchy area.

SHIRTS

The shirt a hiker wears can be thought of as a hiking tool, too. A shirt with large button-down breast pockets is better than most, because it can carry a "pocket" compass (which should in fact be worn around the neck, even when sleeping), a butane lighter, and a small folding knife. (These are the Basic Three tools—covered elsewhere—that are needed to endure even the worst conditions, and they should never leave a hiker's person.) This is another good reason to remind hikers to always button down pockets that can be secured to keep items from being lost.

More preferred by many are the GI-type military shirts with large gusseted, button-down-flap breast pockets and very large button-down cargo pockets at the waist. This cotton-polyester shirt can by itself be transformed into a survival kit, with more than enough room for trail snacks, leather gloves, camera batteries, and so on. Such large pockets also make it necessary to button them down to prevent items from falling out.

In cooler weather, hikers and backpackers have long exploited the fact that unfashionable ("too warm") knit-wool sweaters that grandma bestows on her grandchildren at Christmas will often end up in resale shops in near-new condition. For decades I've purchased warm, water-repellent, practically burn-proof woolen sweaters that had initially sold for as much as two hundred dollars for as little as two dollars.

Whatever your reason for venturing into places where few people go, a roomy overshirt with secure pockets, like the GI fatigue shirt shown here, is a valuable piece of equipment.

Every one of the loaded packs that I've provided to survival clients over the decades have carried a wool sweater. And my personal backpacks have one, too. If you cannot find, or don't want, a wool sweater, knit synthetics (polyester) are very nearly as good; the secret to their warmth is the knit design, which traps a lot of "dead" (warmed and motionless) air while shedding water quickly. Again, avoid cotton knits, which absorb and hold moisture like a bath towel.

JACKETS

Every hiker needs a jacket, whether it's carried inside their daypack or worn because the weather turned cold, windy, rainy, or any combination of the three. Think of this valuable piece of outerwear as a wearable shelter, your go-everywhere protection against hostile elements. You, of course, want the jacket that most possesses protective properties.

A functional spring/summer/autumn (three-season) hiking jacket will have as many large, secure-closure pockets as possible, beginning with breast and hip pockets. It should have sturdy double (left and right) front zipper closures—a backup if one should fail, as they frequently do at the most imperfect times. The zippers themselves should be backed up by a snap closure, because even the best zipper tends to fail at the worst of times.

A hood is essential, too. It ensures that you have at least minimal protection for your head and face. A summer ice or hail storm can be worse than awful to an uncovered head. It doesn't need to be the dead of winter in cold country to feel the sting of wind-driven ice and rain against your skin; the real danger here is that exposure to those conditions swiftly robs your body of heat.

A jacket should be water repellent, but be forewarned that materials like Gore-Tex have not proved to be as ideal on the trail as they were intended (or advertised). Shedding water from the outside doesn't seem to be a problem for such materials, but even in dry weather,

A suitable uninsulated jacket or a heavier coat, depending on the season and temperature, will have lots of roomy pockets to enable it to serve as a wearable survival kit and shelter as well as a hood to protect the head from clumps of snow that fall from trees, from wind and driving rain, and even tree-borne leeches in some jungle forests.

the material retains perspiration on its inside, making a wearer feel damp and clammy. Better to wear a jacket that is less than waterproof, and let the layers under it keep you warm. Being wet isn't immediately dangerous, but being cold and wet for only a few hours is life-threatening.

HEADWEAR

A hat is much more than a fashion accessory to a hiker. The wide-brimmed headgear worn by our forebears since before the Revolutionary War were created to serve as umbrellas, as protection against sleet and hail, and as sunshades before sunglasses were invented.

Nor did a hat's usefulness end there. Many a cowpoke slaked his horse's thirst from a hat filled with water, and sometimes fed his mount from a head pocket containing grain. Likewise, pioneer children used hats and bonnets to contain berries and herbs they gathered. Hats have even been used to catch fish (though this is today illegal under most conditions). Tom Sawyer scared the life out of his Aunt

Shading the sun from your eyes is only one of the uses that make a hat an essential piece of outdoor gear.

Becky when a lump of butter that he'd secreted in his hat began to melt on his head, making him appear to have contracted some feverish illness.

In recent decades, a ballcap with only a brim over the face has replaced the conventional full-perimeter brim, but a diminished brim in no way reduces the hat's importance to a hiker. A ballcap still has the ability to shade vulnerable eyes from the amplified effect of sunlight on water or snow; a ballcap worn low over the eyes will prevent the temporary loss of vision known as snow blindness, which can occur among boaters as well as snowshoers.

A hat can also serve as a prefilter when the only available water source is very murky or filled with debris. By slowly lowering the head pocket into the water until it fills, your hat's fabric filters out large contaminants. Then, when you filter water from the head pocket, having those larger contaminants separated from the water filter's input hose keeps them from being sucked in and prematurely clogging its filter cartridge.

In very hot weather a water-saturated hat of any type has long been used to keep its wearer's head cool. Rinsing your hat in fresh, even silty, water reduces the amount of sweat, salt, and body oils trapped within its fibers. Different hats absorb different volumes of water, based on the materials used in their construction (cotton is very good in this instance), but a hat saturated at every opportunity might mean the difference between heat stroke (or hyperthermia), and a pleasant hike.

DAYPACKS

The first backpackers were Boy Scouts, soldiers, and wildlife biologists; the concept of carrying a backpack as a recreational sport unto itself is a fairly recent phenomenon. Backwoodsmen of old didn't consider carrying the necessities of survival, and maybe a few basic comforts, to be enjoyable or adventurous. When the first hikers began trekking into backcountry places, their uncomfortable frameless canvas backpacks were just a load to be borne if they were to reach, and stay in, those places for an extended period. "Humping" a backpack was not considered to be enjoyable, and rightly so.

Hikers in the twenty-first century have access to the most comfortable, versatile, and best-designed daypacks and backpacks yet created, as well as lightweight, multi-functional gear that would have been the envy of previous generations of hikers.

As woodlands became less common in the latter half of the twentieth century, and every foot of the globe was meticulously mapped by satellites, more people felt an urge to visit the vanishing wilderness, and that prompted a burgeoning market for outdoor gear. Since gear needs to be carried in a backpack, backpacks have long been the subject of continuous innovations on ergonomics, comfort, and utility. That means hikers today can enjoy the finest backpacks ever made in practically any size or color that suits them.

Zippers must be dependable, heavily made, strong, and smooth on both opening and closing. Backpackers and campers agree that the YKK-brand of zipper is best. Also make sure your pack has as many pockets as possible, inside and out. Pockets can be transformed into kits for first aid, food storage, fire-making, or whatever you might need to be easily found. Being able to go directly and quickly to

This twenty-four-liter pack is half the volume of a full-blown adult backpack, but it will carry a lightweight sleeping bag and bivvy shelter, a first-aid kit, survival gear, food, and most or all of the other necessary or just-in-case equipment recommended in this handbook.

whatever you might need, even in the dark, is beyond useful.

The volume of a backpack is generally expressed in cubic liters. How large a pack you select will depend on your physical size, but fifteen liters to twenty-five liters covers the range preferred by most day or overnight hikers. Adjustments of most packs are generous enough to accommodate most hikers. Better to adjust a too-large pack downward than try to fit into an undersized backpack. This is especially true for younger hikers whose bodies are growing rapidly.

There is an old backpacking proverb which states that the amount of gear carried expands to fill the space allotted for it. Resist the tendency to fill your daypack or backpack. Thoughtfully determine what you'll need for the duration of your stay, including survival tools (map and compass, knife, and fire-starting kit) in case unforeseeable circumstances delay your return.

Some daypacks, like this one, are sold pre-equipped as "bug-out bags," with food, water, and the necessities of survival, making them ready to hit the trail with the addition of clothing and hygiene items.

Lastly, but not least importantly, fasten and adjust every strap on your backpack. Movies have made it seem jaunty to carry backpacks over a shoulder by one strap, or to leave sternum (chest) straps and waist belts flopping loose and unbuckled. This is, to put it mildly, just wrong. Backpack manufacturers have empirical (established) data based upon tens of thousands of miles on the trail to draw from when designing their products. Actors on a set are not qualified to dispute them by ignoring features meant to keep a backpack balanced and secure on its wearer's back. An unbalanced or sloppily fitting pack increases the possibility of injuries that could range from a turned ankle to losing your balance on a narrow mountain trail.

LIGHTING

When I was a boy, in the late 1950s and 1960s, the most portable, dependable, and all around best source of light for camping, based on innumerable nights of experience with my friends, was an old-fashioned kerosene-fueled hurricane lantern, so named because it was designed to remain lit in a storm. A hurricane lantern's flame is practically immune to the fiercest wind, and its glass chimney is protected by a wire cage. Even today, many off-grid households rely on this centuries-old lantern design to light the darkness.

Another classic lighting option, preferred if you could afford one, was a pump-up, pressurized, liquid-fuel lantern that burned a fine, continuous spray of extremely flammable Coleman fuel, or white gasoline, into a nonflammable fine-mesh bag called a mantle. The hissing of a Coleman lantern as it radiated a surprising amount of light (and heat) is a

Reliable, dependable, bright, portable LED lights have upgraded the outdoor experience like nothing since the discovery of fire.

Old-fashioned kerosene-fueled hurricane lanterns, like the one that according to legend started the Chicago Fire of 1871 (shown here), are still in use today, lighting remote places where electrical power is sparse, and reliability is paramount.

cherished camping memory for many a grandparent and great-grandparent.

Among hikers and backpackers, portability and weight historically have been common complaints about lanterns (and cookstoves) that run off white gas. But for car, canoe, or kayak camping these still-manufactured, and oftentimes improved, camp appliances are favorites for their efficiency and ease of use. All of the camping cookstoves used by mountaineers and campers in the increasing number of parks where open fires are no longer permitted (Smokey had to get tough!) use pressurized fuel canisters these days, but some can burn regular gasoline, kerosene, even cooking oil.

Be well aware that in actual field trials, especially in snow, more than a few of the fold-up-burner camp stoves have erupted in balls of spraying fire. The "foyer cooking" casually endorsed by camping magazines (that should know better) is never advisable, but if one of the exploding stoves were inside your tent when you lit it, the consequences could be extremely expensive, and maybe painful.

A final type of lantern and stove fuel is sold in prepressurized fuel cans or bottles. Just as the atmospheric pressure increases the deeper you submerge a SCUBA tank, lessening the amount of breathing time it can supply, so does cold temperature decrease the amount of burn-time in this type of lantern or stove. A pressurized can or bottle of propane or butane will deliver its most efficient service in warm summer weather.

When I was a kid, the flashlights of the day used incandescent bulbs that quickly sucked up available energy from low-efficiency dry-cell batteries. The problem was compounded by poorly made flashlights that needed to be smacked against their user's palm when they suddenly went out or refused to turn on at all because subfreezing temperatures had deposited a layer of insulating frost on their contacts. Worst of all, their incandescent bulbs burned out at the darkest and most inopportune times. Many campers or hikers have fumbled with a tiny bulb in pitch blackness, entirely stranded wherever they might be until the bulb was replaced or dawn broke. As with the earliest humans, we learned the hard way that without a portable source of light, the smartest course of action was to make camp right on the spot and wait for morning. There were good reasons that the hours of darkness were once times of quiet and sleep, whether one was a farmer or a battlefield soldier. A twisted ankle or tree branch in the eye could incapacitate the toughest man.

Once they heat up and settle down, all of the multi-fuel stoves exhibited a propane-like burner flame. Never ignite a pressurized liquid-fuel stove inside any type of enclosure or near anything you care about.

Today, the portable lighting problem has been vastly changed for the better. Flashlights, headlamps, and lanterns illuminated by light-emitting diodes (LEDs) are far brighter than incandescent bulbs, use much less energy, and have a working life rated in tens of thousands of hours. While it isn't unheard of for an LED to burn out, on average it will last the life of the lighting unit that it illuminates.

Brightness of LED lights is generally stated in lumens. This is a fairly recent scale—previously we measured brightness in candlepower. Don't let the numbers overcomplicate things; just know that the higher the numerical value, the brighter the light, and the quicker it will drain your batteries. With that in mind, avoid the all-American propensity for bigger-is-better. Two-hundred lumens will light anything you want lighted—including signaling for help at night. More than that is a waste of power in most cases; visibility is limited to just a few yards in a nighttime forest, regardless of a light's

Out with the old and in with new: incandescent-bulb flashlights that had been considered the finest ever made were rendered obsolete immediately following the creation of practical LED lights.

A quality headlamp today needn't require the breathtaking outlay of cash that it did only a decade ago; the fourteen-dollar 3AA headlamp on the left and the USA-made ultrabright rechargeable twenty-seven-dollar model next to it have both passed field trials as well as (sometimes better than) much more expensive models.

Always available, dependable, bright lights in the darkness, both of these low-power, single-AA-battery flashlights are convenient enough to forget that you have them clipped to a pocket.

brightness, due to shadows. And too bright a light blinds companions.

LED lights rugged enough for outdoor use are at this time reliable, (usually) inexpensive, and varied enough to satisfy everyone's needs. Best is a headlamp, backed up by a handheld flashlight. The flashlight can reach into places not accessible to a headlamp, but a hands-free headlamp is more convenient for night hiking.

You don't have to spend a lot of money on lights. A $260 headlamp powered by two AA batteries proved to be just excellent for almost a decade of daily use. But a thirteen-dollar three-AA battery light has more than proved itself in the field, going more than a week of daily use without going dead, and that model has a built-in SOS flash function.

Likewise flashlights don't need to be expensive. Single-AA lights with a pocket clip have performed best, being convenient, bright, and easy to feed. Note that flashlights that use just a single LED have proved more reliable, and equally bright, as models that use multiple LEDs in their heads.

RADIOS

Backpack-able, portable, battery-powered radio receivers have become potentially invaluable for hiking since the latter half of the twentieth century, from the power-hungry AM (Amplitude Modulation) models of the 1960s to today's high-efficiency models that receive AM, FM (Frequency Modulation), and the most-used shortwave bands.

Many packable radios receive NOAA (National Oceanographic and Atmospheric Administration) Weather bands. NOAA's seven national weather frequencies, from 162.400 to 162.550 MHz, are broadcast from local stations nationwide, enabling anyone who wanders away from civilization to have forewarning of weather fronts long before they reach their locations. For a listing of NOAA transmitter station frequencies and their geographic locations, state by state, go to www.nws.noaa.gov/nwr/coverage/station_listing.html, and select the state and area in which you're interested.

Whether used to get up-to-date weather forecasts, hear about national disasters (the author learned of the 9/11 catastrophe from his radio), or just for entertainment, compact radio receivers earned a place in every backpack outfit half a century ago; this AM/FM, nine-band shortwave receiver retailed for under ten dollars when it was purchased.

Reception of most receivers is the best it has ever been, but nearly all incorporate a telescoping chromed-brass antenna to maximize the radio waves they pick up. (Note: this antenna has no effect on AM reception; the AM antenna is inside the radio.) An old woodsman's tool for further enhancing reception is a simple coil (about fifteen feet) of insulated stranded copper wire, with a hobbyist's alligator clip attached to one end. Extend the radio receiver's antenna, attach the wire's alligator clip, and drape the other end of the wire over a nearby tree branch, as high above the ground as possible. Improvement in reception should be noticeable immediately.

A backpack receiver needs to be shielded from the elements, because it will, as a matter of course, be subjected to rain, jostling, and a few knocks. Wrapping your receiver in bubble wrap, then inserting it into a ziplock plastic bag provides adequate protection from almost everything. The bag provides secure protection for your wire antenna, spare batteries, and other small items, and the radio's controls can be operated while it's sealed inside the bag. Protection from the elements has made "shower radios" a popular choice, because these are waterproof, inexpensive, and incorporate a hook that allows them to hang from a convenient branch; the downside is that most are only AM/FM.

Rechargeable-type receivers that employ either—or both—a hand-crank dynamo or a solar panel charging system cost more than battery-only models, and more than two decades of field trials with various models have shown that none recharge well with either system, and some not at all.

BATTERIES

There is no shame, no negative reflection on a hiker's woodcraft ability, if they take advantage of existing technology to make outings safer and more comfortable. In fact, quite the opposite: it goes without saying that Lewis and Clark might have instantly adopted walkie-talkies, flashlights, and MP3 players had those devices been available to them. All of these wonderful gadgets become useless without electrical power, so we must also cover a few important points about batteries.

Field experience has shown the number one rule is that, as much as possible, every electrical device should use the same type of battery. This allows you to steal from one device to power another, and that capability has proved to be very useful. The battery size of choice is AA, because AAs provide the best balance of power and portability.

Alkaline types have the longest life, but they also have one-time use, and when they're dead, they're of no further use. Worse,

With a price tag of less than thirty-five dollars, this all-digital, rubber-armored, AM/FM, NOAA-weather, and shortwave receiver is equipped with a hand-crank dynamo for charging cell phones and tablets, a flexible solar panel that recharges the radio's batteries, and a convenient bag for carrying the entire outfit.

A radio receiver used for hiking will naturally be exposed to environments that are not well suited to electronic devices; an ordinary ziplock plastic bag is both effective and economical protection against the elements.

depleted alkalines are hazardous waste and should be properly disposed of back in civilization.

More popular are nickel–metal hydride (NiMH) batteries that can retain 75 percent of a full charge for up to a year of storage, with two-thirds of the power capacity of their disposable alkaline counterparts, and the ability to be recharged approximately one thousand times.

Battery capacities are measured in milli-amp hours (mAh). The higher their milliamp hour rating, the more power they store, and the longer they will power your device. Ratings from 1,000 to 2,800 mAh are best, with a typical price tag of roughly $2.50 per battery.

MESS KITS

At some point you're going to want a trail meal that's tastier and more nutritious than a granola or fruit bar, and that will require having a mess kit. Simply put, a mess kit is a backpack-able set of dishes that is designed, ideally, to cook foods as well. This is particularly important because freeze-dried meals, as well as dried foods like rice and oatmeal, demand boiling water, even if a meal has the option of being prepared in and eaten from the pouch in which it was packaged.

"Pancake" type mess kits, like the GI mess kit, and those modeled after it, have not proved their worth on the trail. Their shallow, flat pans are adequate to eat from, but poor to useless when it comes to actually preparing even freeze-dried dishes. The shallow dishes inevitably slop liquids over their sides, and attempting to fry in one results in burned food, regardless of whether the pan is aluminum or stainless steel.

With their working life generally measured in milliamp hours, nickel-metal hydride (NiMH), AA-size rechargeable batteries have so far offered the best in all worlds for powering the increasing numbers of devices that have earned their place in backpacks.

THE INDISPENSABLE CAMP SPOON

If you look for an eating utensil set at any website or store, from any manufacturer, you can bet that the outfit will consist of a butter knife, fork, and spoon. The fork and knife are superfluous. The only part of the kit you need for eating is the spoon.

Experience has shown that a spoon is capable of bringing all types of food from dish to mouth—the ultimate goal for an eating utensil. A fork, as anyone who has tried eating peas with one can attest, is a poor choice for doing that, unless a bite must be stabbed, and cannot be shoveled-up on a spoon. A butter knife, even if it's serrated on its end, cannot perform any cutting task that a folding knife can't do better.

Having established you only need the spoon of any three-piece utensil set, we'll go one step further and announce that there is no need to buy eating utensils made for hiking and camping at all. Everything you need is at any local resale shop, and for considerably less than you'd pay at a camping outfitter's store. In a resale shop you'll almost certainly find a large assortment of preowned silverware of every type and size. Of course, what you'll be mostly interested in are the spoons, especially the larger table spoons that are the most popular size among campers and backpackers.

An inexpensive cost also allows you to do something that Mom would likely object to, were you to do it to one of her kitchen spoons, and that is to deform it by bending a small hook into the end of its handle. The hook's primary purpose is to snag the bale (heavy wire) handles of cookpots that have been heated to the point of being too hot to handle—many a hiker has come away with burnt fingers because they underestimated how hot a handle had become. When not protecting fingers from burn scars, the hook provides a convenient way to hang your spoon from a small branch or a similar projection, even a gear loop on your backpack, to keep it out of the dirt.

Available for pennies at resale shops, a table-size spoon is the only eating utensil you need. Bending the end of its handle into a hook enables it to safely snag wire-bale handle pots from a hot campfire.

Better, and usually less expensive, is the nested-pot German-style mess kit. This outfit is the choice of militaries around the world, because it will cook everything, whether living off the land or boiling oatmeal. The kidney shape includes an internal dish with fold-out handle, a pot cover which can also serve as a dish, and a one-liter main cookpot with volume enough to feed two hungry hikers. That space can also be occupied by your next meal, instant coffee, or spices during transport. A bale-style wire handle, which can get very hot from cooking, is easy enough to lift with a knife blade or even a stick. Or with the leather gloves that are always recommended as part of any hiking or long-term backpacking kit.

A few years ago there was a scare among mess kit manufacturers about aluminum mess kits causing Alzheimer's disease (this has since been classified as a myth, per the Alzheimer's Association). Bauxite (aluminum ore) is the most common element on the planet, found everywhere, and it might not be a coincidence that hikers who were frightened away from cooking with aluminum were met with numerous, more expensive options like titanium, stainless steel, nonstick coatings, and so on.

In every instance, a mess kit should be metal, and able to be used over a cookstove or open fire; avoid plastic as much as possible. Prices for a suitable mess kit that will serve you for years to come begin at about fifteen dollars.

Manufactured by a number of companies worldwide, the WWII German-style nested three-piece mess kit has more than proven its value through several decades of survival classes and recreational camping trips.

BUDDY BURNER HOMEMADE CAMP STOVE

In the rural north woods, and particularly here on the shore of Lake Superior, winters are cold, long, and hard. Cold air—known as the Canadian clipper when I was a kid, but now known by the more stylish moniker polar vortex—draws polar air directly from the top of the earth. More than one resident of that area continues to learn the hard way about frozen pipes—especially in the record-breaking cold of recent years.

One very old, time-proven solution has been to place an oversize "buddy burner" in the crawlspace or basement. Many farmers placed a buddy burner under the oil pans of their tractors and other vehicles for an hour before attempting to start their engines, just to heat and thin crankcase oil. And, of course, a buddy burner has long been known as a foolproof, dependable, reusable camping stove.

A buddy burner is essentially a large candle in a metal can. It's made by starting with a cleaned metal paint (steel) or Sterno (aluminum) can with a press-down metal lid. Into the can's center is placed a large woven-fabric lamp wick (asbestos, when it was available, a cotton lantern wick nowadays), long enough to reach from the can's bottom to its top. A length of

Possible to light with a match or disposable butane lighter in the wettest weather, shedding light and heat for hours in even windy conditions, the giant candle-in-a-can called a buddy burner (pint-size shown) has more than earned a permanent niche in the most basic daypack.

fence wire, woven though the wick's length (if necessary), stiffens and holds it from folding onto itself. Another length of wire pierces the wick crosswise, spanning across the top of the can while holding the wick so that it hangs suspended straight from the top of the can.

Finally, with the stiffened wick positioned in the desired location, the can is filled with molten paraffin or even old candles, melted for that purpose. The wax is allowed to cool and harden, then the can's lid is replaced and tamped down to seal it. (Do not replace a lid tightly over molten wax, even after just using it, or the lid will probably pop off explosively, maybe never to be seen again.) Clever hikers even add a book of matches under the watertight lid.

Just as paint cans are made in different sizes, so can buddy burners be made in a variety of sizes to suit different needs. To heat the underside of a house (in a place where it can't cause a fire—exercise common sense), we use a gallon-size that burns for more than a day. As a camp stove, placed at the bottom of a slit trench that's about three inches deeper than the can is tall, a cook pot spanning the trench's top, it works well to heat impromptu meals in the field. Or it can help to light stubborn campfires in the most driving rain. A buddy burner always lights, it can't get too wet to burn, and it would take a hurricane to blow it out.

In an increasingly technical, digitized world, the buddy burner is a primitive, but effective, solution that has worked for me, personally and unfailingly, for decades. And anyone who has had to repair ice-burst plumbing can attest to how much money this most fundamental of space heaters has saved the people who rely on it to keep their home's water flowing.

THE TRENCH STOVE

As common as they've become, lightweight cookstoves suitable for carry in the backcountry haven't been around all that long. When I was a kid camping in northern Michigan, backpacks were simple canvas rucksacks, work boots and hiking boots were the same thing, and cooking a meal in the wilderness was always done over a wood fire. Like so many of the items found in a twenty-first-century wilderness outfit, a practical backpack cookstove just didn't exist.

Yet, it was also prohibitively troublesome to make a conventional campfire every time you needed to cook a meal in the woods. A whitetail hunter heating soup for lunch on a chill November day needed to keep smoke and odors to a minimum, while summer day packers needed only a small source of heat that could be quickly lighted and easily extinguished without posing a danger to the forest. These and other situations, in which a hot meal was desirable but the inconvenience of a fire was not, were addressed with simple affair known as the trench stove.

As its name implies, a trench stove begins with a narrow groove excavated into the ground. One fellow I know calls it a "boot-heel stove," because in softer soils the trench can be excavated by scraping it out with a boot heel. I prefer to do my excavating with a stick, or a machete if I'm backpacking. However you achieve it, the objective is to create a rounded-bottom slit in the earth that's at least six inches deep at its center, twelve inches in length, and about four inches wide. Sides of the trench should be scraped relatively smooth and straight to keep the containment area small and to help direct generated heat.

As with any type of open fire (including camp stoves) be sure to site your trench stove in a place where there's no danger of it spreading via the wind or flammable forest debris. Scrape away flammable materials around the trench to a distance of at least one foot, then use the dirt excavated from it to fashion a low fire wall around the hole's perimeter.

With the trench excavated, the next step is to lay a bed for the fire it will contain. Essentially a platform of dry, finger-thick sticks laid side-by-side to form a floor of sorts at the trench bottom, this bed is needed to shield your fledgling cookfire from moisture in the soil. Without it, moisture vapors from the earth will rise to help extinguish your fire from the bottom, where it actually needs to be the hottest.

After a suitable bed has been laid, you're ready to make a fire at the trench's bottom. Effective natural tinder materials to lay atop the bed include dry pine needles or grasses, reindeer moss, and shredded birch bark. Spread atop the platform in a loose, airy mass, all of these are extremely flammable in dry weather—something to remember any time you use an open flame in the woods. Or, if wet weather makes natural tinders difficult to light, ready-made chemical fire starters like hexamine and trioxane tablets can be had cheaply at Army-Navy stores, and these will ignite at the touch of a match or lighter flame in any weather. The traditional "survival candle," which may in reality range from tea candle to dinner taper, is still one of the best daypack tinders because, used judiciously, a single candle can start dozens of fires. A pint-size buddy burner candle-in-a-can, described earlier in this chapter, accomplishes everything you'll need.

With tinder burning, the next step is to lay a loose cone of kindling sticks teepee-fashion around the flame. Begin with the driest, smallest-diameter twigs available, none thicker than a pencil, and carefully surround the tinder flame with kindling to help contain its heat, shield it from wind, and provide an umbrella against precipitation. Avoid taking kindling twigs from

A buddy burner canned-candle stove is as odorless and leave-no-trace as you can get.

the ground, especially in wet or snowy weather, as these will have absorbed enough moisture to make them hard to burn. Dead, barkless twigs snapped from the trunks of live trees receive less exposure to rain, and their location causes them to shed rather than absorb falling water.

Add more and larger kindling sticks as those below catch fire with a healthy yellow flame. The most common mistake at this point is adding too much wood too quickly, smothering the tinder fire before it can ignite the kindling fuel. Add wood only as quickly as the fire will allow, and when it has become a flaming pile of finger-thick sticks at the bottom of the trench, you're ready to cook.

Using a trench stove isn't much different than cooking with any type of liquid- or gas-fueled camping stove. Simply set your cookpot across the trench, where it will be supported on both sides and kept stable while its center is exposed to hot flames. The trench shape allows the fire to draw all the air it needs from either end, and permits the addition of fresh fuel from either side without removing the cooking vessel. Add fuel as needed using dry, finger-thick sticks broken into approximately six-inch sections, and stir the cooking food frequently, because a trench stove generates a surprising amount of heat.

Like backpacking stoves, a trench stove is much easier to extinguish than a conventional campfire. Just make sure all live embers and smoldering matter has been scraped to the center of the trench's bottom, and refill the hole with the same dirt that came out of it. I also like to pour whatever water is available onto the coals prior to refilling the trench, but even without this somewhat compulsive act, the chance of a buried trench stove reigniting is virtually nil.

Finally, I like to smooth over the fill dirt and literally erase my trench stoves (and campfires) by sprinkling dead leaves, ferns, twigs, and other local debris onto the site. Being buried under six inches of soil makes the odor of fire more difficult for animals to detect, and I believe a covering of decaying leaves helps to further mask and diffuse odors that do escape. Human visitors who come later will appreciate that your fire left no mark on the forest, while seed-bearing topsoil piled onto and fed from below by nutrient-rich ashes will ensure that indigenous plant life returns in abundance—just as it does after a forest fire.

THE BASIC THREE

It speaks well of today's footwear industry that so many folks who tie on a pair of hikers and head into the woods feel ready for anything, but every spring sees a number of hikers who find trouble off the beaten path. Deep, untracked forests where morels, blueberries, and thimbleberries are most plentiful can look very different from one season to the next, and many pickers have gotten turned around in places they thought they knew well. Throw in glacial ridges and hills, dense fog and clouds, a cold rain, wind, a turned ankle, or any combination of those, and a fun outing can become a grueling trial in just minutes. No one who ever got into trouble in the woods saw it coming, and, ironically, the media pays little attention to those who simply weather outdoor emergencies without incident.

The Basic Three (with a few extras), all of which can be carried as a unit on the belt.

(continued on next page)

You don't need to be a survival expert to roam the woods in search of treasures without fear, but you should commit at least as much preparation into wandering far from civilization as you might into going to work or taking a road trip. Most essential for, especially, off-trail trekkers is the Basic Three, a simple outfit that can virtually guarantee your safe return from the woods, come what may.

2

ORIENTEERING

Most animals are born with an on-board organic compass. A ferric (magnetic) deposit at the tips of their noses is attached to neural connections that enable the animal's brain to "feel" the pull of earth's magnetic north pole. We also have a ferric deposit at the tips of our noses, but the sensory conduits between nose and brain are not connected, and it has been proven time and again—sometimes tragically—that humans do not possess a natural sense of direction. This fact may be unacceptable to some, until they really get lost, and those unlucky few who survive the experience will probably never again enter a woods without having at least one compass. (I carry two: a small one on a lanyard around my neck, and a fully loaded sighting compass in the map pouch clipped to my belt.) To help mute the pain of knowing we are always one turn from being lost, this chapter will also include a few handy tricks for determining direction using visual clues from the environment.

History has shown that it's hubris to believe humans have the same sensory compass as most animals.

CHOOSING A COMPASS

No need to be extravagant here, at least not for most single-day outings. All you really need is to know in which direction north lies; every other navigational procedure is based on

All compasses point in the same direction—magnetic north—no matter their cost or complexity.

knowing that constant. By providing a fixed point (magnetic north), a compass enables you to walk the straightest, most unerring line in any direction through any terrain, so you need never get turned around. A hiker practiced in the basics of orienteering can perform some pretty impressive navigational functions using only the most basic compass.

With a more advanced sighting compass, plastic-laminated map, grease pencil, and a bit of basic geometry, you can even plot your precise location on a map by "shooting," or sighting from a landmark whose precise coordinates are known, using a back azimuth (also, "line" or "bearing"). A GPS is great, but don't deny yourself the absolute reliability of a quality compass.

Always trust your compass, perhaps especially when it disagrees with you (again, *Homo sapiens* has no sense of direction). When an orienteer is deep in shaded forest under cloudy skies, with no destination or landmark in sight, it's a very common mistake to doubt one's compass. But unless a compass is obviously, physically broken to the point where its indicator doesn't move correctly, the instrument will never lie to you.

One compass cannot be more accurate than another; they all must point in the same direction, just as water must fall downward, whether it comes from an eyedropper or a bucket. Regardless of expense, every working compass points toward earth's magnetic north pole. More sophisticated compasses have sights for precisely reading the number of degrees between your position and that of a distant landmark, protractors and scales for transferring those angles to a map, and a rotating bezel for fixing direction of travel while hiking.

There are two types of compass movements: liquid-filled and induction-dampened. Liquid-filled is the most popular type, because there's no needle bounce; its indicator rotates to magnetic north and stops there, minimizing the time it takes to get a bearing from a distant landmarks.

The single demerit against liquid-filled compasses is a big one: in actual all-season field use over the past three decades, not one liquid-filled compass of any type or brand has failed to develop a bubble in its indicator capsule after two years of use. Dial-type indicators are largely unaffected by these bubbles, and slide right by them, but needle-type indicators can be stopped by air bubbles, making their readings undependable, and possibly getting you lost if you believe them. With time, and especially if taken to higher elevations, a small air bubble will grow inside the indicator capsule, rendering the compass useless.

Induction-dampened compasses, like the classic GI lensatic compasses, have nothing but air inside their indicator capsules. Reliability is the reason this type remains a mainstay with militaries around the world. Dial-type indicators settle more quickly on magnetic north, but generally take a little time to get there. Needle-type indicators rotate faster, but may take a few seconds to settle. The single problem with induction-dampened compasses is that their indicators may become sticky, even immobile, especially after long-term storage.

Virtually every liquid-filled compass used in the field has developed an air bubble inside its indicator capsule; air bubbles can trap needle-type indicators, rendering the instrument useless, but moving-dial indicators (shown) generally slide right by them.

The next consideration is how well-equipped a compass is for navigation. Simple pocket or zipper-pull compasses (I recommend wearing one around your neck on a string at all times) retail for about ten dollars. As mentioned earlier, these basic compasses point to magnetic north with as much accuracy as the most sophisticated and expensive models. They just lack the sights, scales, and see-through bodies needed for complex and accurate navigational procedures. They'll get you safely out of the woods, but they may have a tough time taking you to a precise location within them.

Map compasses, so called because they're made for use with a map, are equipped with all the tools of navigation. Some are even equipped with Universal Transverse Mercator (UTM) grid scales for use with GPS maps. Within the map compass category are prismatic types that employ a mirror with a sighting line running vertically from top to bottom. By aligning the front sight with the mirror line, then placing a distant landmark atop the aligned sights, you can read both forward (the number of degrees in which the landmark lies from your position) and rear bearings in the compass's mirror.

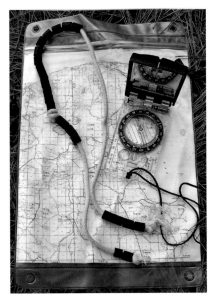

A prismatic compass, like this one, has a mirrored sight that enables you to read both forward and back bearings simultaneously.

A lensatic compass, the most classic of which is the GI compass, works the same way. However, when you align the sights on a landmark, bearing values on the dial are read through a folding lens.

Map compasses come in a variety of styles and prices, depending on quality and utility, but you can buy a very functional compass that will serve you well for under twenty dollars.

Your compass is a valuable instrument, and it should be treated well. And if your main compass should become broken or lost, there should always be a simple backup compass hanging from your neck. With a compass and map, or even a general memory of the terrain you're hiking, you can never be lost in a wilderness. Believe that.

A classic-styled lensatic compass, with sights and reading lens.

USING A COMPASS

A number of survival students have been almost disappointed to find that basic orienteering with map and compass can be learned in a matter of minutes. All any compass really does is point at the planet's magnetic north pole when held flat in the palm, parallel to the ground, so that its indicator swings as freely as possible. Rotating the compass so that its north indicator—and you—are facing north means east is directly to your right, south is behind you, and due west is left.

Like every circle, there are 360 degrees around a compass dial. North is located at 360 degrees, which is also zero degrees, and progresses clockwise around the bezel to east (90 degrees), south (180 degrees), west (270 degrees), and back to north. The four directions divide a compass dial into equal fourths, with 90 degrees between each quadrant. The opposite direction, or "back azimuth," from any point on the compass dial is 180 degrees away from any direction. If the forward azimuth, or bearing, is 30 degrees (less than 180), add 180 degrees to arrive at a back bearing (reverse direction) of 210 degrees; if the forward bearing is 240 degrees (more than 180), subtract 180 degrees to get a back azimuth of 60 degrees.

As this map of Superior National Forest visibly demonstrates, there are very few places on Earth where a hiker is not in a box, so to speak; you are always surrounded by identifiable and hard-to-miss landmarks.

For an average sport hunter or backcountry hiker, all that matters is that a compass keeps one on a straight course. Precise bearing numbers are important in more advanced orienteering techniques, but there are few places on Earth where a person can be more than a day's trek from a marked trail or road—providing he or she knows which direction leads to that trail, and can follow a straight line.

The beauty of a compass, as opposed to the technology-dependent Global Positioning System (GPS), has always been its simplicity and almost absolute reliability. It points toward magnetic north all the time, without batteries or parts that need replacing, it doesn't wear out or rely on satellites, and good ones are at least tough enough for serious field use. Potential problems are avoidable—like the need be sure your compass is

Remember the word NEWS; if you're facing north, east is on your right, left is west, and south is behind you.

not being influenced by nearby metal, whether from a medical alert bracelet or a lightning-magnetized iron ore deposit. Some low-cost compasses can show a tendency to stick, especially in subzero weather (the liquid doesn't freeze, but movements can become tight). Large bubbles in liquid-filled compasses can also be trouble with pointer-type indicators (rotating dials are unaffected), because they can trap the indicator, and keep it from pointing to north. Always check that your compass is operating smoothly and normally by rotating your body back and forth a couple of times prior to taking a bearing. Never attempt to take a bearing within fifteen feet of a vehicle, or any large metal objects.

Just knowing where the four directions lie is enough to keep virtually anyone from making the very common mistake of wandering in circles, and if you can walk in a relatively straight line, few places are more than a day's walk from the nearest road. But if you want to use your compass to get back out of the woods in a place close to where you came in, you'll need to take a "bearing" before you start. That means aligning your compass with north as described above, then using the information it provides to determine which direction you'll be taking into—and back out of—the forest.

For example, if you're about to enter thick swamp from a two-track road, you need to know in which direction that road lies once it and other identifiable landmarks are out of sight. Landmarks like roads, trails, railroad grades, and power lines are the best targets for a "back-bearing" (the direction that leads out) because they span large areas and are difficult to miss. If you leave the road and walk eastward into a woods, then finding that road again is as simple as walking west until you hit it. For most outdoor activities, that's all the orienteering you'll need to know.

Likewise, day activities like hunting and back-country fishing may not need the complexity of precision instruments that are equipped with sights, map scales, clinometers, and other advanced orienteering tools. These compasses are equipped to navigate accurately through any untracked wilderness in the world, but fully exploiting their potential demands more advanced orienteering techniques than are generally needed for getting to and from a camp or deer blind. The keystone of any orienteering outfit begins with a simple "pocket" compass, worn around the neck on a lanyard, and never taken off so long as you are in the woods.

A candidate pocket compass is usually liquid-filled to help its indicator settle quickly, with a movement that turns smoothly, without sticking or jerking. Don't get the idea that simple has to mean low quality, however, because a good pocket compass is as serious an orienteering tool as its more sophisticated counterparts; it just lacks the precision sights and other accessories that most day hikers seldom need.

MAP

The information provided by a compass needs a pictorial reference to maximize its usefulness in the real world, and that reference is a map. Unlike the mid-twentieth-century, when there were still large blank spaces marked "Unexplored Territory" on maps of some continents, today's hiker can know exactly what lies ahead and all around them long before reaching those places.

With compass and map, you can always know which direction to walk to the nearest trail or road, even if you aren't sure of your own position. If you need to cut cross-country, an accurate, as up-to-date as possible map serves as a preview of what lies ahead, terrain that would be best avoided, and where the busiest trails, roads, and thoroughfares lie.

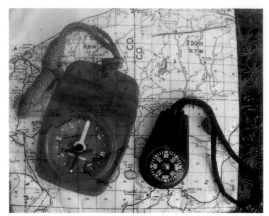

Never disdain a compass because of its small size or lack of complexity; if it points toward magnetic north reliably, it may well prove to be a valuable, even lifesaving, navigation tool.

With a reliable compass and a preferably laminated map (that you can write on with a crayon, then erase cleanly), there are no surprises about the terrain around you.

Any map is better than none, even if it's just a gas station road map. But a topographical map from the United States Geological Survey (www.usgs.gov) will provide the most accurate picture of the surrounding terrain. The difference between a topographical map and other maps is that it shows elevations and depressions in the terrain. Differences in rise above or depression below sea level are displayed as concentric, irregular rings, with the largest ring representing the lowest elevation. Rings get smaller and further inside a feature as elevation rises. Elevation between rings might be represented in feet or yards, depending on the map's scale. Whatever a map's scale, the closer together the rings, the steeper the rise; the wider apart the rings, the more gradual a grade. Downloadable, printable, topographical maps are available online from USGS for a fee of nine dollars.

A digital map on a smartphone or tablet can be relied on until you really need a map, and then your device can be equally relied on to have a dead battery, a broken screen, a software glitch, frosted contacts, to be lost, or to just get drowned in a pouring rain.

TRIANGULATION AND VECTORING

We'd been following a mountain road that wasn't on the maps for hours. Terrain was rugged, and the going was slow, and it was late afternoon when we decided that we'd better get our bearings. None of the three of us had ever been here before, and we had only a vague idea of our location.

One of my companions and I climbed atop a granite ridge, where we could look down onto the surrounding countryside. From there, I could see the bay, and a small lake about a mile inland from it. To its left, I could see a mountain peak whose configuration made it easy to identify on my topographical map. Using the sights on my prismatic compass, I "shot" a bearing to a point on the bay: 45 degrees. The peak was at 326 degrees.

What I really needed to know was not where those landmarks were, relative to my position, but where I was, relative to their position. That meant I had to figure 180 degrees—the opposite direction—from where they were. From the mountain peak—326 degrees—I used a grease pencil to draw a line backward, toward myself, at 146 degrees (326 – 180 = 146). From the point on the bay—45

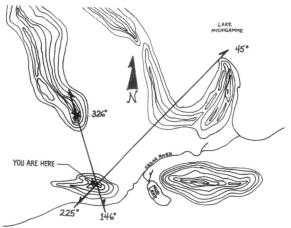

If you can find two identifiable landmarks on your map, you can use a map compass (or any compass, actually) to vector your precise location on a map.

degrees—I drew a line at 225 (45 + 180 = 225) degrees. At the point where those two lines intersected, that's where we stood. You'll note that the forward bearing is at exactly the opposite point on your compass dial, making it a snap to calculate without using any math.

Strictly speaking, this procedure is known as "vectoring," because it doesn't use the three reference points needed for proper triangulation. When you reference from three points, you create a triangle where the lines intersect. Your position is in the center of that triangle. Triangulation is considered more accurate, but vectoring has always been adequate.

MAGNETIC DECLINATION

Earth's true north pole and its magnetic north pole are not in the same place. In North America, that means there is only one longitude, extending irregularly through Minnesota to Alabama, where both poles are in line with one another, relative to the viewer. On either side of this "zero line," the two poles grow increasingly out of line with one another the farther one travels east or west. Confusion occurs because the standard reference point for maps is true north, which at some longitudes can be in a much different direction than the one where your compass is pointing.

In most places, with no more than a few miles from one large landmark to the next, declination differences of a half-dozen degrees are minor enough to be ignored. Ignoring a three-degree declination, for instance, will result in being off-course by only about four-hundred yards at the end of a five-mile hike. In places closer to the pole, where lines of magnetism converge and concentrate, like Alaska, northern Canada, and Denmark, declination discrepancies may be more than thirty degrees, and that is too large a discrepancy to be ignored.

Correcting for declination is simple: Determine, as closely as you can, your actual position on a declination map, which shows in degrees how much difference there is between the two poles. If you are west (left, or negative west) of the zero-declination line, subtract the number of degrees indicated from every compass bearing. If your location is east (right, positive east) of the zero line, add the number of degrees indicated. Some orienteering maps are declination-corrected, printed with longitudinal lines oriented toward magnetic north, instead of true north—be sure you know which, because doubling the declination correction is bad, too.

GLOBAL POSITIONING SYSTEM

What a compass cannot do is tell you exactly where you are. In dense forest where visibility may be limited to only a few yards, even the most sophisticated sighting compass is reduced to merely pointing toward magnetic north. That isn't a problem if you know where you came from and you've kept track of your route, but if you've just survived a plane crash in timber country or had your kayak blown ashore by a typhoon, you might have only a vague idea of your location.

A GPS receives its coordinate data from geostationary satellites that serve as permanent electronic landmarks. By vectoring microwave signals from these fixed overhead beacons, a GPS can calculate its own location to within a few feet from anywhere under that umbrella of coverage. In real life, heavy forest canopy has been known to block signals and prevent the unit from getting lock, as can falling snow or hard rain.

Maps are traditionally oriented toward true north, because the magnetic north pole has historically shifted; within a score of years, the degrees that a north compass reading will differ from the true north on most maps may shift five degrees, maybe more. (Photo courtesy of USGS.)

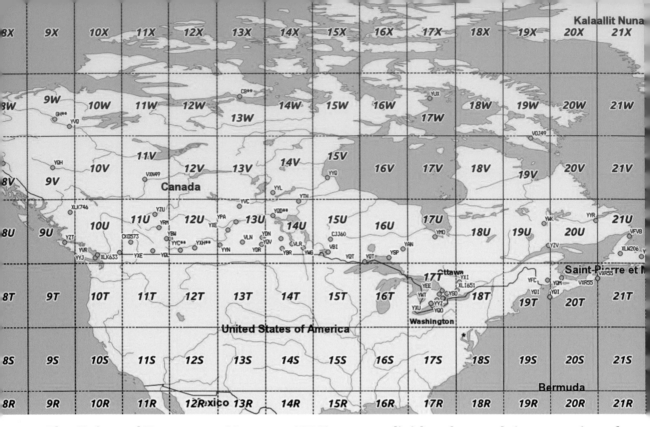

The Universal Transverse Mercator (GPS) system divides the earth into a series of primary squares, each one hundred thousand meters across and designated by a number followed by a letter.

Subfreezing cold is tough on electronics; even with fresh batteries, a few hours of exposure to cold temps can lower voltage below the required operating threshold. Another problem has been frosting of battery contacts—remedied by removing the cover and rolling batteries back and forth under a thumb a few times. Electronics are tolerant of heat up to about 160°F, but temperatures of –4°F can destroy a unit's LCD screen, even crack its circuit board. The best safeguard against cold is to carry the unit in an inside pocket, keeping it as warm as possible.

A handy but potentially hazardous feature of a GPS is its "trek" or "plotter" mode. This function allows a person to wander with no thought to landmarks or navigation, while the GPS keeps track of directions and distances traveled. When its user wants to return, he sets the unit to its "backtrack" mode, and simply follows an arrow displayed on the LCD. This is a useful feature, presuming the GPS remains operational. The danger comes from complacency, because using the plotter mode induces hikers to pay less attention to landmarks and direction. Should the unit be taken out of service, its user is likely to be completely lost.

Be aware that the map grids used to reference GPS and compass readings are very different from one another. The compass references from a geometric scale that divides planet Earth into four equal parts of 90 degrees each, with zero-degrees occurring at the International Date

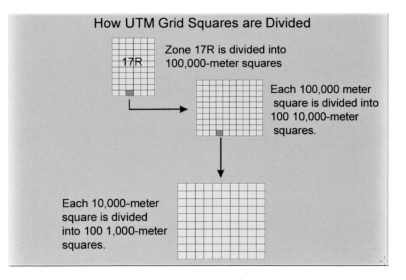

How UTM Grid Squares are Divided

Zone 17R is divided into 100,000-meter squares

Each 100,000 meter square is divided into 100 10,000-meter squares.

Each 10,000-meter square is divided into 100 1,000-meter squares.

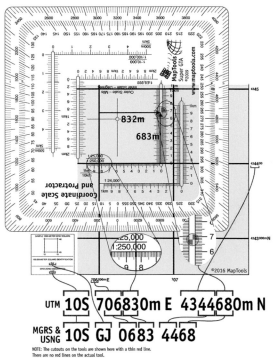

UTM	10S	706830m E	4344680m N

MGRS & USNG	10S	GJ	0683	4468

NOTE: The cutouts on the tools are shown here with a thin red line.
There are no red lines on the actual tool.

The primary 100,000-meter squares are subdivided into ten squares that are 10,000 meters across. Those 10,000 meter squares are gridded into ten 1,000-meter squares and those 1,000-meter squares are gridded into ten 100-meter squares. A GPS receiver can very accurately locate any place on a UTM map.

The survival student's UTM map, printed from software that he'd purchased, was exactly one kilometer off; it took a prismatic compass and topographical map to determine the error. A compass and map are not obsolete.

Line in Greenwich, England for longitude (east–west), and at the equator for latitude (north–south). The large irregular squares formed by intersecting lines of latitude and longitude are subdivided into minutes (one-sixtieth of a degree) and seconds (one-sixtieth of a minute).

A GPS uses a system of sixty north–south grid zones and sixty east–west central meridian lines that begin and end at the same zero points in Greenwich and at the equator. Instead of breaking coordinates down into degrees, minutes, and seconds, the Universal Transverse Mercator grid uses a simpler base-ten system of meters. Depending on how close-up the scale, or "relief," on your map, determining an exact position can be precise to within forty inches.

The bottom line is that both GPS and a compass are valuable to a fully outfitted orienteer. A compass virtually guarantees that you will never be lost, but nothing beats a GPS for finding a remote cabin in untracked winter woods. Maybe the best advice is found on the first page of the instruction manual for Eagle Electronics' Expedition II GPS: "A careful navigator never relies on only one method to obtain position information."

NATURAL COMPASSES

Our species might have been denied the senses and bodies that allow animals to survive where a naked human would die, but our ability to understand and exploit an environment is

unmatched. Where we lack a neurological sense of direction, we have an understanding that some things follow an order that is regular and predictable. Not being able to feel direction, we observe the reactions of other elements that respond predictably to forces from a regular direction. Best known of these natural compasses is the sun, which every kid learns will rise in the east and set in the west for every day of his life. Less known is that Earth's moon follows the same east–west trajectory across the night sky. More importantly, always remember that our sun is directly overhead only at the planet's equator; the farther north one travels, the lower and more southerly the sun is in the sky. Face the sun at any time of day in Ontario, and you will be facing in a southerly direction (the opposite is true when located south of the equator).

Just like our sun, earth's moon rises in the eastern sky, and sets in the west.

If you can see the sun rise, you're facing east–northeast. If your location is north of the equator, the sun and moon must rise in the south-southeastern sky.

In northern and high alpine forests, where viciously cold nor'westers are just part of winter, observers will note that the tops of the tallest conifers are mostly or completely devoid of branches on the north side. The most live branches will be growing from the top's southeast side, where they can serve as a valuable reference in deep forest where the sun might not be visible except at high noon.

Please note: Moss does not grow on the north side of trees; I mention this unkillable myth because to rely on it as true could make a rough situation worse. In fact, in mature northern hardwoods, where only the strongest trees have survived to cover the sky with canopy, north winds can rip through the widely spaced trunks with a lethal chill that prevents moss from growing, except on the protected south side.

Stars have been reliable navigational beacons since the first hominid noticed that they were in almost the same place each night. Fortunately for me, personally, you don't need to have an astronomer's eye or knowledge of constellations to use them for navigation; you just need an open view to a clear night sky and an ability to recognize a few that are most visible. Orion's Belt, a diagonal of three stars running from lower left to upper right, is always visible in the southern sky during winter from anywhere in North America. Likewise the Big Dipper, whose tail is close enough to north to be used as a reference, is easily identifiable.

In the high mountains or in the far north, viciously cold winter wind from the east–northeast stunts the growth of the tallest conifers on that side; as a result, the most healthy and prominent branches on a wind-blown treetop point generally southwest.

THE PACE COUNTER

Another important phenomenon is distance perception. While working as a wilderness guide, I always knew exactly how far it was to campsites and other notable destinations, because that came with the job. But virtually all of my survival students overestimated the distance they'd walked by 200 to 500 percent. A mile through the woods is a very long way, made especially to feel that way because there are so very many landmarks.

Before the days of GPS, which finds a position by triangulating from numerous geo-stationary orbiting satellites, we used a map and compass, but nei-

You can't always see Polaris, the North Star, that represents true north; but the Big Dipper (Ursa Major) is one of the brightest constellations in the northern sky. That's close enough for someone who might have wandered off-trail on a dark night.

ther of these could tell us how far we had actually traveled. It was a simple device called a pace counter that kept remarkably accurate track of the distances we'd hiked.

A pace counter is nothing more than a string of twenty-three beads fitted snugly onto a cord that is at least six inches longer than all of the beads pushed together, with a knot tied at both ends to keep the beads from sliding off. A knot tied into the cord separates the beads into groups of five and eighteen, leaving at least two inches of free space for the beads to slide.

Begin with all beads pushed against the innermost knot, and for every 100 yards you hike (you'll need to determine how many paces that is for you personally beforehand), slide a bead from the group of eighteen to the end of the cord. When seventeen beads (1,700 yards) have been pushed to the end, hike another 60 yards—an estimate is close enough—and slide the final bead to the end. At this point, reset all eighteen beads to their original position, and slide one bead from the group of five to its end of the cord. At this point you've hiked 1,760 yards, or one mile. Repeat the process, sliding one bead from the group of eighteen for every 100 yards of travel, until you've trekked another 1,760 yards, and slide a second bead from the group of five, denoting two miles of walking. And so on, until you've gone five miles, by which point you almost certainly will have ended your journey.

So don't let a solar flare, a nuclear strike, or just battery failure prove to you that a good old fashioned, always reliable system of map, compass, and pace counter is far from being made obsolete by a GPS.

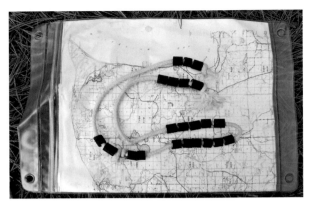

When plotting or following a course cross-country, a pace counter like this homemade version constructed of clothesline and beads of electrical cord insulation, can make keeping track of distances traveled far more accurate.

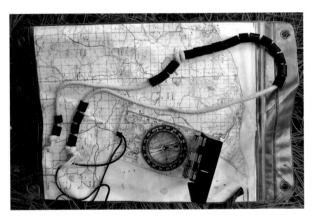

Based on the number of beads that have been pushed to either end of the pace counter's dividing knot, this hiker has walked two miles and 400 yards.

3

FIRE

The survival student had booked a six-day October wilderness survival class, deep within the million-plus acres of Lake Superior State Forest. It was the middle of the Upper Peninsula's late autumn rainy season, and this year was more than living up to its reputation, with nonstop pounding cold rain and temperatures around 40°F. As any veteran of the Vietnam War can attest, it is not possible to stay dry under such conditions, and prolonged exposure to near-freezing rain is the most life-threatening weather a hiker or camper can face.

By the third day, the survival student in question, a fortyish man in good physical condition, had begun to display symptoms of an insidious condition survival

More than any woodcraft or survival skill, the ability to quickly make, safely maintain, and then thoroughly extinguish a fire is most likely to serve you best.

instructors know as creeping hypothermia. The student seemed unable to reassemble his mess kit after a meal, or even to screw on the top of his water bottle. His demeanor grew increasingly lethargic, and he was having trouble understanding what his instructors related to him.

The medical explanation of creeping hypothermia is a very gradual cooling of a patient's core temperature that is not usually marked by shivering, or even a feeling of cold. Symptoms like those just described result as the brain begins shutting down systems that it feels aren't necessary to survival, like cognitive and hand-eye coordination, and even speaking abilities.

The temperature is −8°F in this photo, up from a nighttime low of −25°F; this young man is drying his feet and socks, but several details here illustrate the importance and advantages of having fire.

The condition affects every individual differently, but it appears to occur more frequently in lightly built victims who aren't accustomed to cold weather. Most serious is a tendency for those affected to retire for the evening and never wake up again. Cause of death is believed to be cardiac arrest.

In this instance, nearly a full day away from medical help, it was imperative to restore this student's core temperature to stave off potential tragedy. Survival students have died at schools with a tough-it-out attitude, and his instructor had no intention of adding to that tally. After that, the student was worked hard during the day, making shelter, hauling firewood, digging seepage wells, and warmed by a fire to the point of sweating before bed each night. When the student and instructor parted ways on the seventh day, the student hugged his instructor and actually cried. Never underestimate the lifesaving value that making a fire can have.

Exposure to any temperature below 98.6°F robs a body of heat, and the warmth of a fire may be critical for surviving a not unusual temperature drop of 20°F after sunset. Additionally, the dangerous cooling effect of a hard rain can cause fingers to curl involuntarily into unfeeling claws.

No other use of fire has the lifesaving importance as staving off or remedying hypothermia. An ice fisherman or skater who has just been dragged out of a hole in thin ice doesn't have the life expectancy to warm up the car, or maybe even for an ambulance to arrive. There are many serious reasons for needing fire's emergency warmth, and you can bet that all of them will occur in an environment inconducive to making fire. Troubles are amplified if you're alone and numb, your fingers useless, abdominal muscles cramping as they try to keep vital organs warm, and feeling miserable spasms of uncontrollable shivering that make simple tasks undoable. There is no time to waste with fire-making tools that cannot produce immediate results.

Fire can save you from misery in other ways, too. After Hurricane Katrina, and virtually every other flooding disaster that has occurred in a populated area, an epidemic of cholera, *Giardia*, typhoid, and intestinal cysts like *Cryptosporidium* followed. Boiling water and cooking food kills harmful organisms, and it helps to break down proteins, making food more digestible.

Fire can be used as an emergency signal as well. At night, the glow of a bright fire can be noticed from a dozen miles away, and hot coals covered with wet, rotted wood send an obvious plume of smoke above the surrounding terrain during daylight hours. It's also hard to overstate the psychological value that fire has for making any situation seem less hopeless.

FIRE-MAKING TOOLS

Always keep a disposable butane lighter in one pocket of every garment. Not widely available until the 1970s, this innovation changed the world for outdoors-lovers of all types forever. Liquid-fuel lighters (Zippo, for example) had been in existence since WWI, and they were much used by hikers. But when an inexpensive disposable butane lighter called the Cricket made its debut, with a flaming jet that could be focused onto tinder, thousands of lights in every lighter, and fuel that wouldn't evaporate away, Zippo-type lighters were bested overnight. Butane lighters have consistently remained useful after more than a decade of storage, making it unwise not to have several scattered throughout your backpack and clothing pockets. When their fuel supply is depleted, removing a lighter's protective metal hood exposes its striking wheel and flint, making it a rather anemic spark-thrower that is nonetheless capable of setting fire to frayed tissue paper and cotton balls.

For day or longer hikes, I carry a flint and steel (about fifteen dollars), which has never failed to make fire for me in any weather for more than a decade. Having thoroughly

Natural waters might (and probably do) contain pathogens ranging from *Giardia* to cholera. Making water safe to drink is just one of the many ways an ability to make fire can be beneficial.

A bright signal fire can be visible from miles away at night, while a smoky fire can be seen during daylight.

field-tested a large number of these spark-generators, the following conclusions apply: Get the longest and largest-diameter flint rod available, as the larger the flint (also called a "ferrocerium," or just "ferro") rod, the hotter the sparks. The unit's handle should be large enough to provide a solid grip, even when your hands are wet and your fingers numb with cold. Although popular, the compact little flint rods are simply not up to the task when conditions are wet or windy. Bigger is better in this instance.

A disposable butane lighter makes it easy to light kindling, such as tree lichen.

TINDER

Tinder is the first, most critical step in making fire. The most common mistake beginners make is trying to light a campfire by applying flame to wood that is too massive to be lighted. Every fire begins small, starting with easily flammable tinder materials that burn hot and fast in open air. Burn duration of tinder materials is typically short, but the idea is to use a brief, hot flame to ignite slightly larger dry twigs, then branches, until a hot bed of red coals below provides enough heat to burn the largest pieces of wood.

There is no terrain on which vegetation grows where you can't find tinder for making a fire. Tinders that catch fire with a hot spark or the

When it comes to sparking fire-starting tools, bigger is definitely better; the half-inch diameter flint rod of this Strike Force has never failed to light a fire, regardless of weather.

touch of flame include dried reindeer moss (not really a moss, but a lichen), dead grasses, fine strips of birch bark, or the massed fibers of dead aspen or poplar bark, separated by crumbling the brittle bark from around them. Shed pine needles contain resins that make them burn easily, and even damp ones that won't stay burning can be coaxed by gently blowing the coals to life. The same is true with tiny dry pine twigs found at the end of dead pine branches; one of my survival class demonstrations is to hold a small bundle of tiny dead pine twigs in one hand, and light them into a flaming mass using only a butane lighter. Even in the dead of winter, grass stems sticking above the snow reveal that there are more freeze-dried, flammable grasses below.

Dried tree sap, or pitch, exuded from woodpecker holes and other injuries in pine, cherry, and some other trees, is always flammable, once it has been heated to a liquid state; sap is long-burning and was once used for torches of pitch-saturated grass. A lump of pitch melted onto small twigs with a match is usually enough to set them afire.

If no suitable natural tinder is available, you can make your own by reducing larger pieces of dry wood to more flammable shavings and splinters. The process is as simple as whittling off a small mound of shavings from available dry wood with your knife. The smaller and finer the shavings, the more easily they will ignite. Count on needing a plate-size mound of shavings to create a flame of sufficient duration to ignite larger twigs.

The best fail-safe tinder materials come from your own pocket. Simplest, cheapest, and all-around best of manufactured survival tinders is the fire wick—essentially nothing more than cotton laundry/packaging string that has been dipped into molten paraffin (canning wax), cooled until stiff, then cut into sections and packaged for carry. Some survivalists get fancy, twist-locking or braiding string into thick lengths before dipping to create heavy, long-burning wicks. You can get the same effect from doubling a string several times, and simply tying the combined string into large knots before dipping it in wax. Cotton balls dipped into molten paraffin are also great fire wicks. Wool felt weather stripping, available in rolls from hardware stores, has been a good alternative; it absorbs more wax and burns longer, but is harder to light. With any of these materials, one end or corner of the tinder should be frayed with a fingernail prior to lighting.

Other homemade tinders include cotton balls saturated with petroleum jelly and carried in a pill bottle (too messy, and they tend to dry out), cardboard or cotton flannel saturated with paraffin, or scraps of singed-brown cotton flannel (char cloth, in frontiersman terms) carried in a watertight tinder box.

Military fuel bars, like the trioxane and hexamine used by the American and British armies, are sold inexpensively in Army-Navy stores and catalogs, and either is a must-have for the all-weather fire-starting kit. Made for cooking with a small folding stove, these fuel bars ignite at the touch of a flame in any weather, and burn hot for several minutes, even under pouring rain in gale-force winds.

Dry grass and reindeer moss lichens are very flammable tinders found around the world; latex-impregnated safety tape, found in most first-aid kits, burns easily; chemical tinder cubes ensure fire, whatever the conditions.

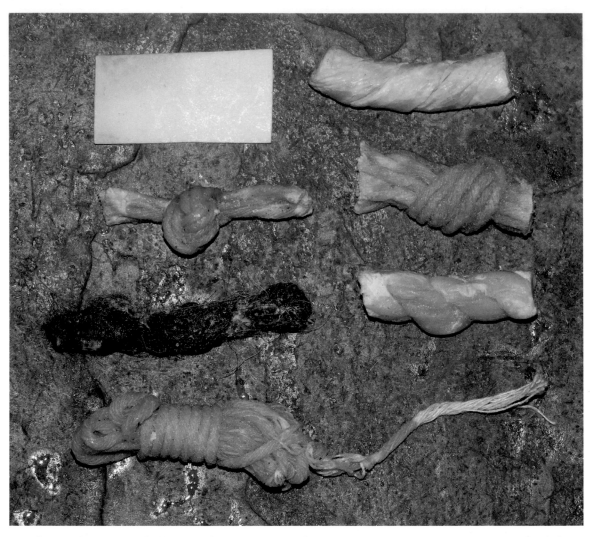

Easily made, never-fail, paraffin-saturated fire wicks are shown here in some of their many forms.

FIRE WICKS: THE NEVER-FAIL POCKET TINDER

The fire wick fire starter is a simple technology for creating a cheap, waterproof, easily lit tinder that has been part of my own survival kits for more than three decades. The fire wick's most basic form consists of thick cotton (laundry and packaging) string that has been saturated with molten paraffin, cooled and hardened, then cut to the desired lengths. The string used must be cotton, not nylon or other synthetics, because cotton burns well and burning synthetics emit noxious fumes. Cotton string can be found in crafts or housewares aisles, priced at about two dollars for one hundred yards.

In the simplest process, a length of cotton string is slowly lowered into a metal vessel containing a pound of paraffin (canning wax) that has been heated to its liquid state. Paraffin is sold in supermarkets for about two dollars per pound. Or, you can melt down the stubs from used candles, which works well for making fire wicks but imparts to them whatever scents or dyes are in the candle wax.

Take sensible precautions when melting paraffin; work in a well-ventilated place where there's no danger from fire. Always wear work gloves when handling hot wax. Never permit a vessel containing molten paraffin to get hot enough to smoke, because that's a precursor to bursting into flames. If the vessel does burst into flames, don't panic. The flaming wax is safely contained; cover the pot with a loose-fitting lid (a tight one will blow off from the pressure) to smother the fire, then immediately turn off the heat. Even removed from heat, paraffin remains liquid for a half hour or so, depending on the ambient temperature.

Cotton string, a pan with paraffin wax (including old candles), a source of heat to melt it, and a cooling container are the basic components needed to manufacture fire wicks.

Making a basic fire wick is as easy as saturating cotton string with molten paraffin.

(continued on next page)

With gloves on, pluck one end of the string from the melting pot using pliers (do this in a place where hot wax drippings will do no harm). Pull the string outward in a straight line, allowing it to drag over the rim of the pot to wipe off excess wax, until the entire length has been extracted. Hang the wax-soaked string over a nail or rail until it cools and hardens—usually about fifteen minutes for single-strand wicks. Longer lengths may be coiled and hung on a nail to cool for convenience.

An assortment of finished fire wicks illustrates some of the forms this no-fail tinder can take.

The cooled strings will stiffen enough to easily cut into sections using scissors. I package the sectioned fire wicks into old pill bottles, or just ziplock bags, and scatter the hundreds I make at a time throughout my possessions. My backpack and survival knife sheaths carry fire wicks, but you'll also find them in my kayak, in my truck's glove box, even in jacket pockets. I also carry them in the toolbox, where they've come in handy for relighting gas furnaces and other pilot lights.

In most instances, a single-strand fire wick is all that's needed, but sometimes I prefer a thicker, longer-burning tinder. For this, I use a twist-lock doubling technique that has been used to make rope from plant fibers since primitive humans discovered that skill. Just twist the string in a single direction until torque causes it to coil around itself when the pull from either end is relaxed. Hold the twisted string taut while folding it in half to bring the two ends together. Slowly ease tension on the doubled string, allowing it to wrap evenly around itself like a small rope. This doubled (or quadrupled if you repeat the twisting process again) cord can then be dipped into molten paraffin, cooled, and sectioned to make thicker fire wicks that burn twice as long.

Alternately, several lengths of string can be bundled together and tied using a single overhand knot. Move a little farther up the lengths (about three inches), and tie them together with another overhand knot. When the lengths are tied together with a series of knots, something like beads on a string, dip the entire length into molten wax, allow to cool, and cut between each pair of knots. The resultant fire starters are nearly as effective as twist-locked fire wicks, and a whole lot easier to make.

Another easy variation uses corrugated cardboard strips cut into sections that fit into your melting pot; leave them immersed for about thirty seconds, until the porous

(continued on next page)

cardboard is saturated with liquid paraffin. After the cardboard has cooled, use scissors to cut the sections almost through, in strips that can be torn loose as needed, like paper matches in a matchbook. The fibrous torn ends ignite with the touch of a flame, and a single quarter-inch-wide strip is sufficient to start a fire under most dry conditions.

An alternative to cotton string is wool felt weather stripping, commonly sold in rolls in hardware stores, or old wool felt pac boot liners cut into strips. Fire wicks made from felt burn longer because they absorb more paraffin, and they ignite nearly as readily as those made from cotton string. Again, use only felt made from

A Fire Wick burning atop snow demonstrates that the tinder will burn under the wettest conditions.

pure wool, not synthetic fibers that not only don't burn well, but emit soot and toxic gases.

To use a fire wick, you'll need an initial source of combustion. A butane or liquid-fuel lighter is a universally recommend survival tool. I've also ignited well frayed fire wicks using only sparks from a StrikeForce flint and steel, but with more difficulty. The most effective method of lighting fire wicks is to fray one end of the wick into an airy mass that flames at the touch of a burning match. Lay the lighted fire wick atop a platform of side-by-side sticks to shield it from evaporating ground moisture. Add fire wicks as needed, and slowly build a teepee of thin dead twigs around its perimeter. Add larger sticks as the fledgling fire grows, until you've achieved a crackling blaze.

FIRE-STARTING BASICS

The first step in starting a campfire is to find a suitable location. When using a shelter, the fire should always be located directly in front of the entrance, but at a distance that will keep flames or sparks from setting the shelter on fire. In windy weather both the fire and shelter should be located on the lee side (away from the wind) of a hill or in thickly wooded terrain to help block air currents that can blow hot sparks into the woods and create a windchill factor in cold weather. As an added precaution, all combustible debris should be scraped or kicked away from the campfire for at least three feet in all directions.

The next step is to create a firepit to help contain popping coals, block wind, and to reflect radiated heat back onto the coal bed, making the fire bed hotter. The traditional method of creating a firepit is to place large stones around its circumference; stones absorb and hold heat from the fire for many hours, and a cold survivalist can use heated stones to keep warm through the night by placing one at the foot of a bedroll, or even hugging a large one against his belly.

Be warned never to expose stones taken from a stream bed to open fire; it rarely happens, but I've seen water-logged stones heat and explode like a grenade. In lieu of stones, excavate the fire pit to a diameter of about eighteen inches wide by six inches deep, and arrange the excavated soil into a low fire wall surrounding the pit's perimeter. Remember Smokey Bear's slogan: "Only YOU Can Prevent Forest Fires."

While not always necessary (snow or sand country) or feasible (experienced campers seldom cut their firewood to convenient lengths), a firepit is always recommended when there is any chance of a campfire spreading to the surrounding terrain.

STARTING A FIRE

The next step is to lay the fire in preparation for lighting; begin by placing the tinder—which can be a mixture of different materials—in the center of the firepit. A platform of finger-thick dead sticks laid parallel on the ground gives your fledgling fire a head start, allowing it to develop a hot coal bed before making contact with wet earth; this is especially important when there's snow on the ground. Once a good coal bed has been established, a fire—insulated from below by its own ashes—will just melt away the snow around it until it reaches bare ground, but a platform is essential to efficient fire making. Lay your tinder in a loose, airy mass in the center of the platform.

With a wooden platform to keep your fledgling fire off the ground, a loose mass of flammable tinder (reindeer moss lichens, in this case), and a pile of small kindling sticks at the ready, you can start your fire.

Next, lay a tipi of small, dry sticks, none bigger than a pencil, all around the circumference of the tinder pile so that they come together and support one another about eight inches above the floor of the firepit. This cone-shaped picket of kindling helps to hold the tinder from blowing away, and provides an umbrella for the tinder fire, while allowing maximum exposure of each stick to flames. The tipi method of arranging kindling will ensure a sizeable air gap exists between the tinder pile and the sticks above it, as well as between the kindling sticks themselves.

When the woods are wet, you might use a manufactured tinder (fire wicks, trioxane, or hexamine) for the initial stage, using it to dry then ignite waterlogged natural tinders, which in turn burn long and hot enough to dry and ignite the kindling tipi. Take kindling sticks for the tipi from the trunks of standing trees, some of which will always have dead twigs attached within easy reach. Shielded from rain by foliage, and suspended in open air, dead twigs still attached to trunks are always driest, whereas those lying on the ground are likely to remain damp for weeks. Wood from the ground is fine for a campfire that has a self-sustaining bed of coals—in fact, wet, rotting wood thrown on hot coals is good for signals, and the smoke also acts as insect repellent—but starting a fire requires having the driest kindling you can find.

In wet or inclement conditions, you might want to use a waterproof, long-burning fire wick (cotton batting wrapped in cotton string, in this instance). Fire wicks, and various ways of making them, are covered in the sidebar on pages 51–53.

With platform, tinder, and kindling tipi in place, apply a flame to the tinder, either directly using a match or lighter, or with a lighted fire wick or other combustible material. A good flint and steel, like the StrikeForce, permits the grip and pressure needed to strike sparks hot enough to ignite even damp tinders. Add more tinder to the base of the tipi until the tipi sticks begin to flame hotly, then carefully add more sticks, one at a time, so as not to smother the still weak flames. When a solid bed of red coals has formed atop the platform, begin laying progressively larger kindling sticks lengthwise and parallel to one

After lighting the tinder on its insulating wooden platform, you're ready to carefully add very small kindling sticks.

another atop the coals. Gently blow into the red coals until they glow hotly, causing the fresh sticks to smoke, then flame. Continue adding more wood until the parallel furnace pile is as large as you need it to be.

A loose, airy mass of kindling sticks (not necessarily a teepee form) placed atop the burning tinder catches fire, inviting larger fuel as it burns to coals.

SPLITTING KINDLING

Should it become necessary to split a piece of wood into smaller strips using a knife blade, there is a way to do it that not only protects your knife, but it can be accomplished using the most lightly built folding knife and hand pressure (you don't even have to be strong).

Place the cutting edge atop the end of the wood to be split (it doesn't matter if the end is sawed-off flat or jaggedly broken) and press it down gently but firmly into the grain with a wiggling motion. Maintain a firm grip on the wood, so that a sharp blade can't slide down far enough to contact your hand. When the blade is embedded a quarter-inch or so, rock it back and forth gently to drive it more

You can use a knife to easily split a piece of wood.

deeply, then twist it sideways to cause a split to develop in the wood. Using only hand pressure, push the blade deeper into the split and rock the knife's blade to widen the separation. At this point, a twist of the wrist will usually cause the wood to split in two.

Do not try to split off too large a strip—maximum size is largely dependent on the size of the knife being used and the leverage it provides. When splitting kindling to make a fire, narrower and thinner is always better in any case. The smaller the tinder or kindling, the more easily it will catch fire. Again, be especially cautious to not drive the sharp knife edge down into your skin. Wear gloves if possible.

Finally, knife manufacturers and survival experts do not recommend that you hammer knife blades through wood—a recently popularized practice known as batoning. It is unsafe, damaging to the knife, and unnecessary if you follow the procedure detailed above. You can read more on this in chapter 4 (see pages 68–69).

GETTING FIREWOOD

Where you can start a fire, there will probably be fuel to sustain it, but available large-diameter, long-burning logs will not be in convenient lengths. Do not waste energy trying to break large wood to fire-size lengths. The simplest method is to lay the ends of two or more large trunks onto the coal bed from opposite sides, parallel to one another. As the ends are consumed, feed each length further into the fire. Alternately, you can burn lengths in half, but if the length is elevated at either end, be prepared for the fire to burn down under and away from the log; you might have to keep adding wood from below before large ones burn in half.

Forests are constantly shedding dead branches, and there should be an abundance of smaller branches on the ground, along with a few wind-sheared tree tops and an occasional whole dead tree. Drag lengths to your fire butt-end first, so the natural upward angle of still-attached branches helps to keep them from snagging against other trees. On deep hardpack snow, all firewood must come from standing trees, and sometimes standing dead trees will have rotted enough to be pushed over and dragged back to your fire.

A lot of contemporary hikers have broken knives trying to hammer them into wood to split it; as this series of photos illustrates, even a folding knife can split kindling safely without endangering its blade or using a hammer.

When there's snow covering the ground, you obviously can't pick up firewood from the forest floor; that leaves standing dead trees and dead branches.

Be sure to lay in a good supply of wood before making camp each night, because, even if you have a flashlight, there is a potential for injury in untracked woods. In some places, you could walk off a cliff, turn an ankle, or suffer a twig to the eyeball.

THE HEATING FIRE

Fire generates heat, and how a fire is arranged determines how much. Many cold nights have proved that, once a hot bed of coals is created, laying firewood lengths side-by-side atop them is most efficient. Seen end-on, the stacked wood resembles a pyramid, and it can be built higher and hotter by adding more wood, of almost any length or diameter, to the pile. This type of heating fire throws its heat to either long side. That heat can be used even more efficiently by placing yourself between the fire and any solid surface, at least three feet high; this reflector can even be made of snow.

THE COAL BED

A coal bed was once used by mountain men to help keep warm during frigid winter nights, when a five-point wool blanket was a standard bedroll. A coal bed prevents a sleeper from getting cold by providing a constant, slowly diminishing source of heat from below. A coal bed will keep a person warm throughout the night, even with a light bedroll in –25°F, as I can personally attest.

The first step is to build a long, hot fire that measures approximately four feet wide by seven feet in length, using a small shovel or entrenching tool, or even a slab of wood. The fire should be fueled until a two- to three-inch bed of red coals forms. The glowing bed of coals is then covered with the loose dirt you removed from the hole and tamped down. An alternate method is to excavate a shallow, body-length depression and then shovel hot coals into it, covering them with the dirt taken from the excavation.

The dirt-covered coal bed can be used without further work, but I've learned that the normal rolling and shifting of position that occurs during sleep can brush away protective earth and bring the sleeper to a rude, painful awakening. As protection against this, I lay a thin layer of pine boughs or leafy branches over the dirt, and cover them with a poncho or ground sheet.

COOKING FIRE

Cooking over an open fire makes a fool out of most skilled gourmet cooks. The most common mistake is trying to cook over a flaming campfire; a campfire generates greater heat than a kitchen range, and food cooked on flames tends to burn on the outside before it cooks on the inside.

A fire made using the "furnace pile" configuration of parallel logs provides at least one flat, heated spot on which to set a cooking vessel. Flames forced through gaps between burning logs make ideal range burners. Larger logs do not burn away below a cooking vessel and cause it to spill, and focused heat blasting up from between logs is easier to cook over. Bear in mind that you can't regulate heat, so you regulate exposure—if food is cooking too fast, move it farther from the heat.

A spit is a traditional way to cook small animals; it doesn't require any cooking vessels, and is the easiest way to cook game in a survival situation. A spit begins with two forked sticks driven vertically into the ground on either side of a firepit.

A furnace pile configuration allows for a steady, hot fire that can be built up as needed (even getting hot enough to temper steel), and provides plenty of stable, flat surfaces on which to place a cookpot.

The straight, bottom end of each stick should be pushed at least six inches into the soil, and both should be stable enough not to fall over under the weight of the loaded spit. The Y-shaped joints of these support sticks should be approximately two feet above the floor of the firepit. The sticks should be made from green wood, although dry wood can be used as long as the sticks are placed far enough from the fire to keep them from catching fire.

The spit itself should be constructed of green wood at least an inch in diameter and long enough to extend beyond the joint of either support stick. The spit is sharpened on one end and threaded through the rib cage and the pelvis for small mammals. Small birds or fish are simply speared through the ribs and slid over the spit. Larger fish are spitted by piercing them at an angle near the tail, bending the body into a U and piercing again near the head. I recommend against using pine woods for a spit, as these can taint food with a taste of turpentine.

Suspend a spitted animal or fish over a low fire by setting the end of the spit into the joint of the support stick at either end and sliding the meat to the center of the spit. The fire beneath it should be kept low, and the meat turned frequently. Cook all wild meat or fish completely, and never eat raw wild game or fish, because most species can carry parasites.

Wilderness cooking is just one of the activities in which leather work gloves are a useful tool. Leather gloves offer protection when working around burning wood. They aren't impervious to fire, but they enable quick handling of burning wood or hot cookware, as well as protecting against cuts and slivers.

USES FOR ASHES

When boiling wild plants to eat, add a tablespoon of wood ashes to the water. Adding wood ashes to soups is a tradition among indigenous American cultures. An Odawa friend told me that his grandmother used to sneak a spoonful of wood ashes from the fireplace into cookpots when his mother wasn't looking. American pioneers thus learned to use lye made from ashes to hull corn for hominy, making it easier to digest. Modern science has revealed that caustic elements in wood ashes break down tough plant cellulose, allowing the human digestive system to convert indigestible proteins into usable amino acids. An ability to enhance the digestibility of tough plants (and meat) broadens your food choices, and helps to get the most from plants you eat.

BANKING A FIRE

Aboriginal humans have never extinguished their camp fires unless they were leaving the place for a long time. In real life, putting out the fire to go hunting for a day was impractical, and possibly unwise, because it would be needed again that evening, and conditions might not be so agreeable for making fire by then. The trick was to "bank" the fire so that it neither burned nor died out but smoldered idly and could be quickly rebuilt into a warm blaze. This uncomplicated, but seldom described, technique involves little more than half-smothering a bed of hot coals with one or more large-diameter logs placed side-by-side on top of them. Good banking logs include wet, rotting trunks that are too big and damp to catch fire, but can slowly dry and smolder just enough to keep the coals below hot. Just roll the logs over to expose hot coals that can be used to ignite tinder by gently blowing them to flaming hotness. When restarting a fire from coals, remember that dead coals placed atop red coals will reheat to red-hotness from contact. Left for too long, the banking logs will smolder away from the coal bed, until the gap between them is too great, and the coals starve.

THE SIGNAL FIRE

A signal fire differs from a cooking or heating fire in its size and intentional high visibility. It has to be large and bright to attract as much attention as possible from as many miles away as possible. The heat and sparks generated by such a big fire precludes it from being located anywhere near a shelter or other flammables. Bluffs, open beaches, and other clear, preferably high places are among the most visible and safe choices for locating a signal fire.

Banking a fire allows it to idle and smolder, maintaining hot coals for two days or more that are unable to flame, but ready to be coaxed into a campfire by rolling over the log and adding kindling sticks.

To be as effective as possible, a signal fire must be as large as it safely can be, and it will consume a great deal of wood quickly. For that reason, the tall tipi-shaped pyre is probably best preassembled and left ready to be lighted from a smaller fire nearby. Construction of the ready-made signal fire begins with a hot-burning tinder, such as dried grass, topped by a large tipi of dried twigs and sticks of a fast-burning softwood. Next comes a larger tipi of heavier branches about six feet in length. The two tipis will help keep the tinder dry by forming a roof over it. When the survivalist spots a plane or some other potential rescuer, he lights the tinder, which lights the smaller tipi of sticks. The flames from the smaller tipi will in turn ignite the larger tipi, sending a brilliant pyre of flame into the night to a height of ten feet or more.

Assuming that both tinder and wood are dry, the signal fire will flame up very quickly, usually within minutes. But be warned: the larger tipi will consume itself from the bottom up and can be expected to burn for no more than fifteen minutes before collapsing to one side. For this reason the signal fire must be located in a place where there's no danger of causing a forest fire when it falls over.

A bright tipi-style signal fire, placed in a high, open location affords maximum visibility and provides a beacon of light to observers from miles away at night.

Flames become far less visible during daylight, but a plume of smoke can be seen rising above the forest from many miles distant, and there are always people who are alert for potential forest fires. An added benefit is that smoke is perhaps the most effective insect repellent.

During hours of darkness a signal fire can be seen for miles, but in daylight the flames fade to near obscurity. Watchers who man fire towers know that flames from even the hottest forest fire are difficult to see in full daylight, but a plume of smoke against the sky is highly visible. Adding to the detectability of a signal fire is the recent fact that more and more fire-prone forests are under constant infrared observation by geostationary satellites.

Armed with this knowledge, one can continue to signal during the day by building a large, bright fire at night and then partially smothering it with a layer of damp, rotting wood or wet leaves during the day. The coals will have enough heat to burn the damp material but not enough to ignite it, and the fire will smoke heavily.

THE SAFE CAMPFIRE

A fire warms the body and soul, lights the darkness, makes hot meals possible, repels animals and biting insects, dries wet clothing, and provides an effective means of signaling for help in an emergency. The hissing blue flame of a propane or liquid-fuel cookstove just doesn't have the same hypnotic effect that a crackling wood fire has, and old-timers can appreciate that a stove outfit weighs a heck of a lot more than a fire starting kit.

Unfortunately, campfires have become politically incorrect because a few campers have improperly managed their fires. Used correctly, a campfire does no harm and can become an island of lush new growth in a few months. Used carelessly, though, a fire can burn uncontrollably through thousands of acres, so practicing this art has become problematic in many places.

The first rule of campfire-tending is always dig a firepit. Unless you're camped on solid rock or beach sand, never simply build a fire atop the ground, but always lay it in an excavated hole about two feet in diameter by roughly eight inches deep. If you can accept an extra three pounds, an E-tool (folding shovel) makes digging a firepit easy. My own SP-8 Survival Machete (made by Ontario Knife Co.) works nearly as well, and in a pinch, you can even use your belt knife. Be prepared to sharpen any edged tool you employ for chopping through roots, sand, and dirt.

One caveat about the fire pit is that it must always be excavated in dirt (i.e., nonflammable soil). In a few places, like northern Michigan's cedar swamps in summer, dry, peat-like sphagnum moss can extend several feet below ground level. History has already shown that a fire in such terrain can smolder below ground, traveling slowly for perhaps a mile before springing to life as an inferno. Be careful of your environment.

Soil excavated from the firepit is best formed into a low wall around the pit's perimeter, where it provides extra containment. Leave about a quarter of the wall open to facilitate cooking and fire tending, and to help maximize the amount of heat radiated.

In cold weather, I wrap a fire-heated stone inside a towel and then shove it to the foot of my sleeping bag, where it keeps my toes warm all night. Never place any rock taken from water in or near a fire; stone is porous, and when it remains submerged for an extended period, it absorbs water. Exposing a waterlogged rock to fire causes moisture inside it to expand rapidly in the form of steam, sometimes building sufficient pressure to explode the stone into sharp, hurtling fragments.

After excavating and walling the perimeter of the firepit, clear a firebreak at least four feet wide all around it by scraping any flammable material into the firepit. This ensures that popping embers find nothing to ignite.

Keep your fire small for most purposes. A large fire is too hot for cooking, which is best done on a bed of coals, and the bigger the fire, the more airborne embers it generates. And it's also easier to spot, should you want to remain unobtrusive.

Never locate your fire under tree branches; always be sure it has a clear chimney to the sky. Aside from the obvious fire hazard, subjecting live overhead branches to smoke and heat does nothing to promote their health. Likewise, site your fire at least six feet from trees and saplings that might be ignited by heat from the sides.

HOMEMADE CAMP STOVES

And, as mentioned in chapter 1, a buddy burner has long been known as a foolproof, dependable, reusable camping stove. It is essentially a large candle in a metal can that can be easily transported and contained. See a description of how to make one on pages 23–24.

Essentially a giant candle in a can, a Buddy burner has served for generations wherever a source of heat has been needed.

4
THE ESSENTIAL KNIFE

Every animal has cutting, digging, tearing, and stabbing instruments in the form of teeth and claws, because an ability to do those things is necessary to survival in the wild. Today, movies and the media have succeeded in making the working-size knife worn by several millennia of frontiersmen into an object of suspicion, even derision. But knives are useful tools, and you should always have one when hiking.

There is no wrong knife, only knives of varying quality and function. Paramount is that a knife feel comfortable to its user, and that will be a different knife for different people. Many prefer a Swiss Army–type knife, but in that class of cutting tool I like the superior versatility of a stout multi-tool on my belt or clipped inside a hip pocket until needed for light cutting chores. Designed to perform a variety of jobs, multi-tools tend to sacrifice a little function, but no knife is bad when you need to cut, whittle, drill, or gouge something. Quality multi-tools start at less than fifty dollars.

For outings that are longer than an hour, and more likely to take adventurers farther from civilization, a strong, fixed-blade sheath knife is

Since the first human stood upright and learned that a sharp rock could cut things, a knife has been standard equipment for aboriginal tribes, pioneers, and anyone who ventures off the beaten track and away from civilization.

appropriate. From the WWII-designed US Air Force Survival Knife, to Gerber's Light Multi-Functional Mark II survival knife, a stout belt knife is as valuable today for prying, chopping,

A few examples of multi-tools that are likely to earn a place in the hiker's backpack.

and digging as it was when a dirk-size sheath knife was part of every rural dweller's daily apparel. Some, like Schrade's versatile "Extreme" survival knife line, have the makings of an entire basic survival package, with gear pouches in the sheath to accommodate fire starter, compass, fishing tackle, and other small necessities.

THE BLADE TRINITY

Once, I was asked why I carry so many knives while camping. I had, at the time, a fixed-blade survival knife and a working-class jackknife on my belt, as well as a heavy, short machete strapped onto my backpack. I laughed, because I'd answered this question before, and replied, "I have as many as I need." It would be hard to find a survival instructor, or any experienced outdoorsman, who didn't believe that a good knife is the cornerstone of every wilderness kit in any environment. With a strong, keen blade, you can cut a rope, fashion and whittle a multitude of tools, and perform countless chores that would be tough to impossible without one.

But experience has proven many times that no single knife is ideal for every job. The trustworthy fixed-blade that friends say is welded to my hip in the woods suffices

(continued on next page)

for everything, but it isn't the most effective tool for delicate tasks, like filleting bass, or digging out slivers. Neither does it deliver the chopping power or leverage to efficiently clear brush and make kindling. I could get by with only a survival knife, but this versatile trio of working knives is worth the weight when quality of life depends on the gear in my possession.

Two examples of the blade trinity.

The beauty of this triad system is that, with some limitations, any one of these knives can perform every task. A hardcore backcountry backpacker will find plenty of uses for all three around camp, but will probably carry only a survival knife and folder for day hiking. At night, or for in-camp activities like fishing, the belt knife might be left in a tent, while the handier folder serves to cut fishing line, clean a bass, or open a new blister-packaged casting reel. This three-knife outfit ensures that you will always have the ideal blade for the task at hand, and it guarantees that you will have a functional knife on your person at all times.

HIKING FOLDERS

There are few jobs that a small knife can perform that a large knife can't do as well or better. Even so, there's a good reason that surgeons perform operations using a scalpel rather than a butcher's knife. From picking splinters to draining blisters to shaping a new tent stake, there are just some cutting chores that need the fine touch and delicacy of a sharp, precisely controlled blade.

Folding knives have evolved far past the original iconic Boy Scout knife, with an awl, bottle opener, and can opener. Those tools have become less important in an era of tear-open foil packs, pull-tabs, and little need to sew sailcloth or leather. Here are a few of the points that have proven most important in a folding knife that's qualified to be carried into the backcountry.

An example of a classic Scouting knife, CAMC4A. (Knife courtesy of New Mexico Scouting Museum. Photo by Bob Wick.)

You don't have to go broke buying a good folder. This knife retails for under fifteen dollars and passed a two-year field trial with flying colors.

First, understand what a folder's job is. It's not a camp knife, and it should never be used as a prybar; the tough chores are for the fixed blade hanging from your belt. A folder's purpose, among other light cutting chores, is to fillet fish and to whittle marshmallow sticks. Make no mistake, a folder can and will eventually break if you abuse it unnecessarily, no matter how it's made.

A traditional configuration, with blade and handle on the same axis, is the best performer. The blade's point should be in line with the center line, to make it easier to control, less likely to slip under pressure, and more able to drill a neat hole.

A secure lock to keep a blade from closing on its user's fingers is one important improvement over the old slip-joint folding style. There are numerous designs for keeping a folding blade in the open position, but except for personal preference, there's no real difference in lock strength; all of them will keep the cutting edge from coming down on your fingers.

Newer-style knives also have pocket clips attached to their handles. This permits a knife to be carried securely in a hip pocket, so it can be reached easily without digging into a pocket, and carried without the inconvenience of also needing a belt pouch.

BATONING

In the past decade or so, there has arisen the apparently previously undiscovered practice of "batoning" a knife blade lengthwise through a piece of wood; using a larger piece of wood as a bludgeon to split it into smaller pieces.

I mention the practice here only to say that it is not only entirely unnecessary, but stupid to hammer the blade of what is perhaps your most vital survival instrument into a chunk of wood. In half a century of living in the wilderness, I have never found occasion to commit this act of abuse, and neither did any of the past masters of woodcraft—including Daniel Boone, Jedediah Smith, and Davy Crockett. Batoning is the invention of neophytes who, in the twenty-first century, have few legitimate daily uses for their knives, like butchering meat and making tool handles. Some method of determining how good or bad a knife is had to be created, so the practice of batoning firewood was invented.

And that wouldn't matter, except that driving a knife blade through wood with a heavy club will break it. Maybe not the first few times, but no knife alloy can withstand

(continued on next page)

that level of abuse for long without a large, usually half-moon shaped chunk of its blade breaking away. Ironically, the poorer the knife (i.e., softer and less able to keep a sharp edge), the longer it can typically survive being hammered, so if the practice is supposed to be evidence of good quality, it usually proves the exact opposite.

Manufacturers of working-class lumberjacking axes specifically recommend against pounding the tool's head into wood, and if batoning is considered a bad idea for an axe, it's definitely not a smart thing to do with a far more lightly built knife.

Should it become necessary to split a piece of wood into smaller strips using a knife blade, there is a way to do it that won't destroy your knife: Place the cutting edge atop the end of the wood to be split (it doesn't matter if the end is sawed-off flat or jaggedly broken) and press it down into the grain with a wiggling motion. When it's embedded a quarter-inch or so, rocking the blade back and forth while twisting it sideways is sufficient to cause a split to develop in the wood.

Using only hand pressure, push the blade deeper into the split and rock the knife's blade to widen the separation. At this point, the wood will usually split in two. Do not try to split off too large a strip—maximum size is largely dependent on the size of the knife being used and the leverage it provides. When splitting kindling to make a fire, narrower and thinner is better in any case. Be especially cautious to not drive the sharp edge down into your skin.

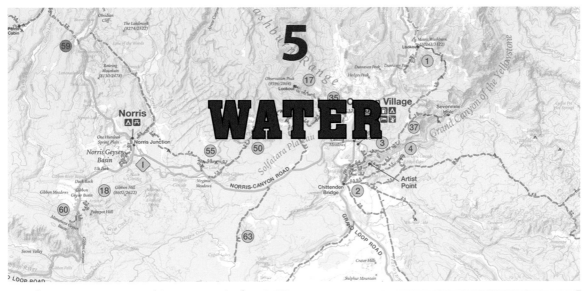

5
WATER

Drinking water is critical in any survival situation, because no one can live more than a few days without it. Water is necessary for cell reproduction, to flush toxins from the bloodstream, to maintain a functional body temperature in both hot and cold temperatures, and to digest food properly.

The first symptom of dehydration is dark yellow urine, often with a musky odor of concentrated toxins. Worsening symptoms can include constipation with dry, ball-like feces that are difficult or impossible to pass without outside assistance (usually a finger, even when being treated by a doctor); diverticulitis, accompanied by abdominal pain and nausea; and intestinal blockage

No one lives more than a few increasingly miserable days without water, and there are a multitude of ailments that stem from not getting enough to drink.

with headache, fatigue, fever, and, lastly, a slow, unpleasant death from toxemia (blood poisoning) and renal (kidney) failure. It's best to stay hydrated, especially when hiking in the wilderness away from immediate medical attention.

WATER FROM PRECIPITATION

Rain or snow that falls through a smog cloud that often hangs over industrialized places is known to contain airborne pollutants like sulfuric acid and industrial chemicals, resulting in precipitation that can actually damage the paint of automobiles it falls on. But no pathogenic organisms are known to exist in falling precipitation.

The volume of precipitation collected can be increased by spreading a poncho or tarpaulin at a slight horizontal angle, then placing a vessel under its lowest point to catch runoff. Absorbent clothing—especially cotton—may be used to collect and coarsely filter rain by wringing water from saturated fabric into a container.

Fresh snow is safe to use as drinking water, but "hardpack" snow that has lain on the ground for several days or longer, or ice covering bodies of water, may contain dormant and still infectious parasites. To avoid gathering snow that might harbor parasites left there by or washed there from animal feces, take only the first one to two inches of powder for drinking water, and try to boil whatever snow you use for cooking or drinking purposes.

THE DANGERS OF UNTREATED WATER

The Food and Drug Administration estimates that 370,000 Americans contract waterborne parasites annually, and the Centers for Disease Control and Prevention claim that 80 percent of us will be afflicted at least once within our lifetimes. Parasites are not exclusive to developing nations or to the poor, and they are much more common, and more easily contracted, than is generally believed.

Feces are the source of most parasites, whether aquatic or terrestrial. Most land animals do not defecate directly into their own drinking water, but runoff from melting snow and rain guarantees that eggs (oocysts) from parasites will be washed into streams and lakes, just as they have adapted to do.

One in every thousand Americans contracts a waterborne parasite every year, and every case is a miserable, often dangerous, experience that is best avoided.

Most parasites are contained in scats left by infected animals; parasites are then washed into waters by rains and snow runoff, where they lie in wait for a new victim to drink them.

Science is still discovering parasites that can live in a drop of natural water, but three that campers and backpackers in North America should be most concerned with are *Giardia lamblia*, *Cryptosporidium parvum*, and *Cyclospora cayetanensis*. Digestive tract parasites remain infectious year-round and are not killed by freezing. In addition, the US Fish and Wildlife Service has issued warnings that tapeworms, which are not aquatic, might still be contracted from waters on Lake Superior's Isle Royale National Park, as their eggs are washed there from infected wolf scats. In some tropical climates, you can add to these heart, liver, and lung flukes (worms) that even today kill thousands of people each year.

Waterborne pathogens are not killed by freezing but can lie dormant for months encased in ice.

The greatest human fear of waterborne pathogens stems from their microscopic size and our inability to detect their presence. Not every sip of water harbors parasites, but all streams, ponds, or lakes contain them. Flowing water is not parasite-free, regardless of current speed or remoteness. The only safe natural water sources are spring heads, where subterranean water flows directly from the earth, and even then only at the source, before the spring has flowed far enough to be tainted by runoff from surrounding terrain.

Adding to the arcane nature of parasites, two or more hikers might drink from the same waters and only one will become infected. Explanations could be that one did not ingest from a school of parasites, or his immune system was strong enough to repel invaders before they could get a foothold in the intestines. Some people may become immune to parasites they've already survived—a good argument

Most aquatic parasites are carried to water from infected feces by rain or snow runoff, and no body of water on Earth is free of them.

for maintaining a strong immune system—but even an adapted immune system can be overwhelmed if the number of parasites ingested is high.

CHEMICAL WATER DISINFECTANTS

Iodine tablets are still widely sold as water disinfectants in camping supply and Army surplus stores, but they are not recommended for serious survival because they do not kill some of the most dangerous parasites. Iodine kills bacteria (typhoid, cholera), flagellates (*Giardia*), and viruses (hepatitis), but not cysts (*Cryptosporidium*) or flatworms (tapeworms)—the latter of which may be infectious as eggs or as free-swimming flukes. Chlorine—sometimes sold in the form of halazone tablets—kills viruses and bacteria, but not cysts or all flagellates.

Recently obsoleting both those chemicals as water treatments are chlorine dioxide tablets made from a cocktail of sodium chlorite and sodium dichloroisocyanurate dihydrate, like the Micropur MP1 tablets from Katadyn. Each Micropur tab treats one liter of water, killing giardia, bacteria, and viruses within fifteen minutes, but requires a four-hour wait to ensure the demise of tough cysts.

Similar to Micropur tablets are new electro-chemical purifiers, like MSR's MiOx, which promises "municipal-grade" water in the field. The MiOx uses watch batteries to ionize a chamber filled with untreated water and salt, converting those elements to chemicals that are safe for humans, once diluted as directed, but lethal to pathogenic organisms. According to microbiologist Lisa Lange, the superoxygenated solution is a cocktail of antimicrobial chemicals that will kill all organisms within a liter of water, although a four-hour wait time is needed to ensure the demise of cysts. Because these purifiers can quickly and continuously treat large volumes of water, they have become a standard for disaster-relief operations.

While neither chlorine nor iodine are proof against some of the most common aquatic pathogens, chlorine dioxide tablets can kill all dangerous organisms in water. (Photo courtesy of Katadyn North America.)

DISINFECTING WATER BY BOILING

An age-old method of killing all aquatic pathogens is to heat the water they inhabit to a rolling boil for one minute. In reality, virtually every organism will be killed before the water reaches 180°F, but the boiling point of 212°F provides visual confirmation that a lethal temperature has been reached. The Environmental Protection Agency (www.epa.gov) confirms that even heat resistant hepatitis viruses (rarely encountered in nature) are killed after boiling for one minute.

WATER FILTERS

The downside of treating water with chemicals or with heat is that neither removes or reduces toxins. Germs and parasites can be made harmless by killing them, but in the aftermath of a disaster, it can be expected that even natural waters will be polluted with heavy metals, fertilizers, pesticides, and petrochemicals. The most convenient tool for addressing this problem is a backpack-type water filter, and I believe one of these should be in every kitchen and automobile, as well as in every backpack.

Boiling suspect water has always worked to kill harmful pathogens, but does not reduce or remove heavy metals or chemicals that contaminate the groundwater of many urban places.

Simply speaking, a water filter uses external pressure to force untreated water through a semipermeable cartridge whose pores are too small for bacterial and parasitic pathogens to penetrate—a process known as "reverse osmosis." Some do this with a two-stage pump that draws in raw water, then drives it through a filter cartridge; some do it by squeezing water contained in a flexible bottle through a filter; some use the force of gravity to push water through a filter element under its own weight. Some have ceramic filter cartridges, some are made from paper and fiberglass. All water filters are manufactured following EPA guidelines that require they remove bacteria, cysts, and flagellates, and they also strain out up to 80 percent of harmful chemicals. They do not remove submicroscopic viruses, but these are seldom encountered away from civilization, and are easily killed by additional treatment with chlorine or iodine. Some water filter kits include viricide chemicals, either in a stage of the water filter itself, or in a separate bottle.

Which filter is best depends on the intended use. Paper-filter models are least expensive, and slowest to clog because of increased surface area, but they have an average life of two hundred gallons. Ceramic filters are much easier to clog with silt, but the unit can be disassembled, the filter cleaned, and put back in service in a couple of minutes. Ceramic filters have an almost infinite use life (they do need to be scrubbed with the abrasive pad provided to clean them), but can break if dropped onto a hard surface. Squeeze-bottle filters are excellent for traveling light, fast, or—especially—by small boat, because you simply dip the bottle into raw water, screw on the cap with attached filter cartridge, and squeeze the bottle to obtain potable water from its drinking tube.

Almost the stuff of science fiction, MSR's MiOx purifier uses untreated water, ordinary salt, and electrical current from wafer batteries to create a superchlorinated cocktail that is lethal to all harmful organisms in natural water.

Disassembled for drying after a trip afield, MSR's MiniWorks water filter with long-lived ceramic cartridge is representative of the reliable simplicity that makes modern water filters a must-have in the home and the backpack.

Invented almost a century ago, the portable water filter has truly come into its own only in recent years. (Photo courtesy of Katadyn North America.)

DISTILLED WATER

Distilled water is the result of using heat to evaporate water into water vapor, then channeling that gas into a confined space where it cools, recombines, and condenses back into liquid water, but without any impurities. This is the same boiler-condensed water that previous generations used in electric clothes irons to allay buildup of mineral deposits that might clog steam-ironing vents and younger generations might know from science class. Distilled water is also the same stripped-down, tasteless hydration sold by the millions of liters to consumers every day in North America alone.

Simplest and lightest of portable water filters is the personal all-in-one squeeze bottle type; just fill it with untreated water, and squeeze potable water from the drinking spout. (Photo courtesy of Katadyn North America.)

Distillation as described above can be performed in the field in a still. Being lighter than particulate matter, the gaseous water rises, leaving everything else behind, then condenses to form pure water after cooling. The advantage of a water still is that it can transform sea-water, sewer-fouled flood waters, extremely toxic coolant from automobile radiators, scummy pond water, even mud, into potable water.

BASIC SOLAR STILL

The simplest distillation devices, manufactured solar stills have long been standard equipment for US Navy life rafts, and they have been recommended in virtually every wilderness survival manual in print. A solar still uses the sun's warmth to evaporate untreated water, trapping water vapor against a transparent or translucent waterproof membrane. There the vapor cools and condenses back into water, which drips into a container below.

A solar still can be as uncomplicated as digging a hole in the ground, setting a metal soup can at its bottom, and covering the hole with a sheet of sturdy clear plastic, like that used for covering lumber. As daytime temperatures cool after sunset, water vapor trapped by the plastic membrane condenses against its underside. A weight (for example, a stone) placed in the membrane's center makes it cone-shaped, and gravity causes condensed droplets to slide down-ward into the container below.

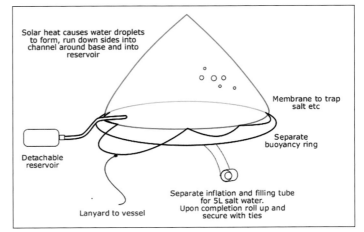

Solar heat causes water droplets to form, run down sides into channel around base and into reservoir

Membrane to trap salt etc

Separate buoyancy ring

Detachable reservoir

Separate inflation and filling tube for 5L salt water. Upon completion roll up and secure with ties

Lanyard to vessel

Solar stills that can convert seawater into enough potable water to keep a downed flier hydrated and alive indefinitely have been standard issue for US Navy pilots since WWII, and today are more efficient than ever. (Image courtesy of AquaMate.)

A solar still is most effective when constructed with a clear plastic membrane that permits maximum sunlight to penetrate, and it works best in arid conditions, where air isn't saturated by evaporated moisture. Under desert conditions (hot, dry days and cool nights), a solar still—or several of them—can keep a person alive.

CONDENSATION STILLS

A more efficient variation of the basic solar still is the solar condensation still. Start by filling an enclosed container—a metal or plastic gasoline or jerry can with a pour spout is ideal—half-full of contaminated water, leaving sufficient air space to allow maximum condensation. Slide a four- to six-foot section of garden hose over the can's pour spout; in most instances the hose will fit snugly without modification, but it may be taped or hose-clamped to the spout to help ensure that no vapors can escape except through the open end of the hose. Wrap the hose into a single coil, tying or taping it to hold that form. Make sure the coil is at the bottom (see illustration at right) to permit gravity to trap any heavier than air particles that might somehow be forced into the hose. Finally, set the half-full container onto a roof, or any other sunny, hot surface, and place the end of the hose into a collection container.

Whether heated by the sun or over a low fire (metal cans only), condensation stills can be made from just a six-foot length of hose and almost any spouted bottle or container—including two-liter soda bottles. Any of these will deliver a constant supply of drinking water so long as the water inside is evaporating.

HEATED CONDENSATION STILL

A solar still is passive, reliant on sunlight and humidity levels, but a heated condensation still uses applied heat to actively evaporate contaminated water, enabling it to continuously produce drinking water. This condensation still is fundamentally the same as the solar type, except that it requires a steel gasoline or other metal can because it uses the heat of a low fire to actively evaporated untreated water. Again, the can's pour spout serves as an output for condensed water, and should be lengthened with a garden-hose extension that is long enough to accommodate a loop for trapping particles that might be forced into the hose by heat.

Because it can operate nonstop, twenty-four hours a day, for as long as fuel and untreated water are available, a heated condensation still is ideal for producing drinking water for a group. Safety warnings include never heating water to a boil, and never permitting the container to go dry. Both conditions could cause unsafe pressures to develop inside the container, causing it to split at its seam or even to explode. If the can begins to bulge even slightly, remove it from heat immediately.

THE SEEPAGE WELL

More than one piece of survival literature advises that it's better to drink untreated water than to die of thirst. That's debatable; petrochemicals and other toxins found in urban floodwaters can cause serious illness by themselves, and having a parasite under conditions that already tax bodily resources to the limit can be lethal. The best course of action is suffer neither malady.

As this sixteen-year-old cabin well illustrates, a seepage well is simply a hole dug straight down to the water table.

Seepage wells have been used since the first human settlements were built. Known in lore as a village well, the nexus of community gossip, or in fables as a "wishing well," the seepage well is simply a hole dug straight down to the water table. Like a springhead, water that fills the bottom of the well pit is cold and potable because it has been filtered through may tons and feet of soil where no parasitic organisms can live.

Although well diggers might have gone the way of the telegraph, the practice of digging a well is as viable today as it ever was. Even the most urban vacant lot in New York City can yield water if you can dig down to it. The trick is to find a place where water is close to the surface, and not inaccessible under bedrock or another impenetrable layer.

DRIED WATER HOLES

African elephants know that places where water had pooled in the rainy season can still provide a life-sustaining drink. Low places where water had collected, from dusty river beds to ponds that have dried up under a hot summer sun, often have water just below their surfaces, protected from evaporation by an insulating layer of sand or dried mud. Like a seepage well, digging down in a low spot at the bottom of a dried riverbed—usually identifiable as a ditch-like slot in the earth—will often reveal wet soil, and beneath that, water. Look, too, for scales of dried mud that have cracked and curled upward from what had once been a pond bottom, or sand that has been arranged in concentric waves by lapping water that has since evaporated; you can often find water just a few inches below these places.

Dried, cracked silt-mud atop sand tells of standing water having recently been there, and the water table probably lies no more than a foot or two beneath the surface.

WATER FROM AUTOMOBILE RADIATORS IS NOT POTABLE

A documentary on a respected TV channel suggested emergency drinking water could be obtained from automobile radiators if it was strained through a cloth and then boiled. This small error is an example of how survival instructors have a responsibility, a duty even, to their students to be correct or else be silent. The chemicals diethylene glycol (DEG) and ethylene glycol used to make antifreeze are lethally toxic even in minute quantities, and there are slower-acting poisons from the lead-solder joints that seal radiators and their copper cores. Nor would I recommend trusting radiators containing "nontoxic" propylene glycol unless there were no alternatives. These poisons cannot be boiled away or adequately removed by a backpack-type water filter (although a filter will reduce chemical concentrations by up to 80 percent). Unless you are going to distill it, water drained from the cooling or heating systems of any engine are not safe for making drinking water.

CANTEENS AND WATER BOTTLES

In a world where millions of resealable, unbreakable, water-tight plastic containers are discarded every day, suitable canteens are everywhere. Chances are good of finding at least one beverage bottle in any car or truck, in garbage cans and dumpsters, and along roadways where some motorists incomprehensibly continue to toss empties from car windows. Wash bottles as thoroughly as possible, and use only food-grade containers, because plastics are in fact porous, and may absorb poisons that were in their original contents.

Ready-made canteens include the G.I. one-quart canteen, canvas case, and steel cup outfit that served well from WWII through the Vietnam War; this belt-carried system enables its owner to boil and cook with untreated water, then to transport it in a case that can be wetted to keep its contents about 20°F cooler than the outside air. Nalgene hiker bottles are lightweight and wide-mouthed to be better suited to freezing temps that block narrow spouts with ice. The newer stainless steel bottles also enable boiling of suspect water, but bottles and screw caps need to be tied together to be survival-ready. Or you might opt for a water bladder that can contain up to two liters of water yet rolls up small enough to fit into a hip pocket when empty. Tips to remember with all of them is that half-filled canteens are advised in subfreezing temperatures, because sloshing water doesn't freeze easily. But also remember that the sloshing of a canteen can be heard by other people and animals nearby.

In a real pinch, wetted rags, cotton clothing, even saturated foam rubber can be placed into a snack or other plastic bag. The bags themselves might not be sealed enough or sturdy enough to transport while completely full of water, but the absorbent material is kept saturated by

Excellent canteens don't need to be bought, as these eighteen-year-old juice bottles clearly illustrate; in fact, purpose-made water carriers are often just a waste of money.

Wide-mouth bottles are better for use in freezing temperatures, where bottle necks can become blocked by ice.

impermeable plastic walls. To get a drink, focus a funnel from the bag opening into the mouth or into a container, and squeeze the bag to press water from the absorbent material inside.

CONSERVING WATER

Never try to conserve drinking water, especially if your survival strategy entails traveling on foot. Desert hikers have been found dead of dehydration while carrying filled canteens, having denied themselves water until they were overcome by the effects of thirst and heat. Much like the cooling and heating systems of an automobile, a human body cannot operate efficiently at reduced fluid levels, and forcing it to do so is flirting with potential breakdown of the whole machine. The best place to transport water is in your stomach, and the best strategy is to use what you need, then concentrate on finding more.

STORING WATER

Storing water long term is a prudent strategy for remote cabins, seagoing boats, and even the most urban apartment. With terrorist threats looming over populated areas, most governments today recommend their citizens store sufficient water and other commodities to endure several days without utilities. Having water on hand can be particularly critical in large cities, where an interruption of municipal utilities not only means loss of water for drinking, cooking, and bathing, but for disposal of bodily wastes that can turn the most modern metropolis into a disease-ridden ghetto inside of a week. In less dramatic events, it makes good sense to stash just-in-case caches of drinking water along hiking trails, or arid sections of trails, where water might prove to be in short supply.

If you're thirsty, and you have water, drink it. Hikers have died of dehydration while attempting to ration water. (Photo courtesy of Katadyn North America.)

Storing potable water is simple and virtually free; plain tap water has proved drinkable after eight years of storage in plastic fruit juice bottles in the corner of a basement. According to most survival authorities, basic drinking water requirements should be estimated at two gallons of water per person per day. In most instances an individual's bodily needs will range downward from there, but never forget that water is also needed for bathing—disease may be one result of long-term lack of hygiene. Water will be needed for cooking and washing dishes, to refill toilet tanks for flushing, and for cleansing wounds. As vital

Storing water is a critical, yet simple and inexpensive, safeguard that anyone can take to prepare for almost any contingency.

as water is to life, and as critically scarce as it has proved to be in so many actual disasters, it would be difficult to have too much potable water stored.

Containers for storing water are abundant and inexpensive or even free. Plastic jerry cans, usually colored blue to designate them as water cans, are made for water storage, and some even have spigot valves in their caps. Heavy-duty plastic juice jugs are ideal for water storage, and their smaller sizes ensure that only a small amount of water will be lost or contaminated if a container is breached; those same qualities make these containers well suited for use as canteens while traveling. Plastic soda bottles are acceptable for storing water but not as rugged.

Avoid storing water in opaque plastic jugs, like those used for milk and some juices; these are extruded from a plastic that is made with corn starch to make them biodegradable, and they will begin leaking in a few weeks. And never store water, or any consumable, in any plastic container that once held toxic substances; although they may be waterproof, plastics are actually porous, and most will absorb minute quantities of poisons stored in them.

Probably the best method of storing tap water is to fill a container with hot water right to the rim of its mouth, then screw its cap on snugly. As the already sterile hot water cools, it will contract minutely, creating a vacuum that ensures its contents cannot be contaminated, and effectively "canning" the water inside.

Raw or untreated natural water should be boiled or otherwise purified before storage. Again, filling storage bottles with hot (not boiling) water is most effective for sealing out contamination, and you can safely add three drops of tincture of iodine or chlorine bleach per liter to ensure the demise of bacteria or viruses. A simpler method is to drop a sodium chlorite tablet (not to be confused with sodium chloride) into each liter of untreated water being stored to ensure that all pathogenic organisms inside are killed.

Stored drinking water should be kept in a cool, dry place. There is no chance of algae or any other live organisms growing in containers that have been filled and sealed according to the preceding instructions. Cool, dry places (basements, closets) are probably the best storage spaces, but the only real concern is to prevent water from freezing, which could cause containers to split. Check water stores at least once a year, inspecting containers for leaks or damage and replacing them as needed.

6

HIKING FOODS

Many survival authorities downplay the importance of staying well fed in a survival scenario, because, theoretically, it takes about three months for a healthy human being to die from starvation. This bad advice disregards the problem of hypoglycemia. When a typical modern human being says "I'm starving," what they really mean is that they missed dinner. Many people, especially in North America, have never known what it's like to forcibly endure hunger for days at a time.

Depletion of available blood sugars demands that one's body switch over to burning body fats to keep it going. This is known as "hitting the wall" by marathon runners, but for most people, it's called hypoglycemia. Symptoms of this condition can range from dizziness and nausea to outright loss of consciousness. I can't count how many survival students I've seen go to their knees—and even fall into a fire on one particularly cold and rainy day. The cure is as simple as restoring the energy to the blood with quickly absorbed foods, then keeping it there with slower-burning foods, like rice, oatmeal, and cheese.

So, you see, it isn't about whether you're tough or strong. It's about staying at maximum efficiency in an environment that does not favor the weak. Low blood sugar means a compromised immune system, and that means susceptibility to diseases, infection, and other ailments that a well-fed body might shrug off.

Whenever you're engaged in any high-energy outdoor activity, you need to eat regularly to keep your body and mind operating at maximum efficiency.

A frequently cited USDA recommended minimum daily calorie requirement is 2,000 calories. But that determination is based on a normal man in a normal environment. A snowshoer, for example, can burn in excess of 1,000 calories an hour. Updated USDA estimates range from 1,600 to 2,400 calories per day for adult women and 2,000 to 3,000 calories per day for adult men. Estimated needs for young children range from 1,000 to 2,000 calories per day, and the range for older children and adolescents varies substantially from 1,400 to 3,200 calories per day, with boys generally having higher calorie needs than girls. Within each age and sex category, the low end of the range is for sedentary individuals; the high end of the range is for active individuals.

THE HUMAN DIET

Talk about the proverbial muddied water. There are so many fad diets, so many "superfoods," and so many dietetic secrets to losing weight, living forever, and achieving the libido of a bunny rabbit that any sensible person might just throw up his hands and eat fast food for the remainder of his life.

In truth, mother nature has a whole lot to teach anyone who'll pay attention. A carnivore is endowed with the canines necessary to rend flesh. *Homo sapiens* has small canines, like chimpanzees, that do eat flesh, but not primarily. *Homo sapiens* also possesses grinding molars, for masticating tough plant tissues. A naturalist might say that humans are therefore evolved by natural selection to eat a modicum of meat with their vegetables.

Americans especially eat too much fat in their normal diets. Fat tastes good to us, as does sugar, and an abundance of either, or both, in processed food increases the desire for, and sales of, such foods. It is the objective of companies to increase revenues, and that means producing goods that consumers want to buy. Our taste buds consider energy-rich foods desirable, even to the point of eating too much of them. In a world where lives have become less labor-intensive than they've ever been, it doesn't help that food manufacturers add fats to everything.

Hikers of today have the option of eating a hot, self-heating meal like this one anytime, anywhere, without the inconvenience of a camp stove or making fire.

But the opposite of eating too much fat is malnutrition, and that, according to the journals kept during the Lewis and Clark Expedition (1803–06), can be outright debilitating. Symptoms range from general weakness and malaise to chronic dysentery and a compromised immune system that can make normal mild injuries and ailments severe enough to be life-threatening. The Lewis and Clark party curbed their symptoms by drinking their supply of tallow (animal fat) candles, melted down for them after the famous Shoshone girl, Sacajawea, recognized their deficiency. At first, the men were repulsed at the idea of drinking melted rancid fat, but once they began to give their bodies what they were craving, they drank up their entire candle supply.

Keeping one's body healthy is a fundamental of basic survival that cannot be overstressed. Fad diets have no place in an environment that might demand a supreme effort.

Bone marrow is a superfood (predators, including domestic dogs and cats, love it), but humans tend to turn up their noses at eating it.

MEAL, READY-TO-EAT (MRE)

I once wrote several article-length reviews for a "maga-log" published by Brownell's, and in it they wanted a review of MREs (Meals, Ready to Eat). I had my doubts, because previous forays into the land of premanufac-tured meals have not convinced me to give up my old standby survival foods, like rice, beans, oatmeal, and preblended baking mixes. Military MREs tasted olive-drab; as one soldier put it back in the 1980s, "The best tasting part is the toilet paper."

Times have changed, and MREs have vastly improved. The several meals that I've tried have not only been palatable, but indistinguishable from their canned super-market counterparts. There are currently numerous brands and types of MRE available.

The United States Marine Corps issue meals reportedly provide about 1250 calories per meal (13 percent protein, 36 percent fat, 51 percent carbohydrates). Hermetically sealed heavy plastic envelopes are said to withstand drops from up to 98 feet. Shelf life is usually ten years, when properly stored. There exist approximately twenty-four meal variations—although, that is always subject to change. Typical contents are listed in the sidebar. The

Five miles from the nearest back road, 1.5 miles from the North Country Hiking Trail, and soaking wet from a pouring rain, a nutritious ready-to-eat MRE was just the thing for restoring expended energy.

downside to this otherwise excellent choice in survival foods is that military MREs are the most expensive of all of them.

TYPICAL CONTENTS OF A MILITARY MRE:
(MRE 40 Menu 2 in Parentheses, pictured at left below)

Entrée, typically spaghetti or beef stew (beef shredded in barbecue sauce)

Side dish, like rice, corn, fruit, or potatoes (black beans in seasoned sauce)

Crackers or bread (tortillas—plain or chipotle)

Spread—peanut butter, jelly, or cheese (jalapeño cheddar cheese spread)

Dessert—cookies, candy, or cake (cookies—oatmeal, oatmeal chocolate chip, or oatmeal chocolate chunk)

Beverages—fruit drink mixes, cocoa, dairy shakes, coffee, tea (lemon-lime, orange, or tropical punch)

Hot sauce or seasoning, optional

Flameless chemical-type ration heater

Spoon

Accessory pack—Safety matches, coffee, creamer, sugar, salt, chewing gum, hand wipe, toilet paper

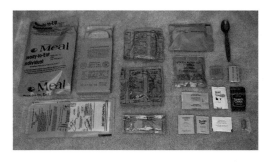 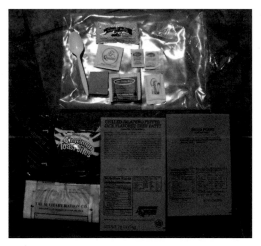

Today's Meals, Ready-to-Eat (MREs) are varied, tasty, and even self-heating, making them ideal for hikers and long-range backpackers. On the left is an example of a US Military MRE Menu 2; on the right is an example of a private sector MRE. (Photo credits: Ashley Pomeroy (CC BY-SA 4.0), Voodoo Tactical.)

FREEZE-DRIED FOOD

For grab-and-go situations, consider the freeze-dried offerings from companies like Mountain House and ReadyWise. Just add water to reconstitute a wide variety of dishes that are sometimes hard to differentiate from fresh-cooked. Heating is optional with many recipes.

Freeze-dried foods are packed into featherweight Mylar/foil, vacuum-sealed, tear-open pouches of two or four servings each. As ReadyWise's Blaine Furner noted, smaller individual pouches help safeguard against loss and spoilage. Shelf life of freeze-dried fare is almost a moot point. To quote Mountain House's R&D manager, Norm Jager, "We're not just guessing that our products will last over thirty years, we know it."

Available individually, in sampler boxes, or stackable polyethylene buckets that can feed one person for one to two months, meals like these are less expensive than fast foods (and more nutritious). Prices vary with size and assortment. Purchased individually, single-entree pouches of anything from spaghetti and meatballs to beef stew cost around six to eight dollars, depending on contents, and some come with their own chemical-type, water-activated heater. Buy in bulk for better deals.

If you have water and heat, freeze-dried foods may be prepared in and eaten right from their own envelopes. Such meals remain edible in a backpack for at least twenty-five years, and may be the ideal choice for hikers.

DEHYDRATED FOODS FROM HOME

Beans

I have stored dried beans—pinto, navy, kidney, and black—for more than fifteen years. A month ago, I made ham and bean soup from a variety of beans that were twelve to fifteen years old. The beans had not been hermetically sealed, but packed, in their original bags, inside cleaned one-gallon plastic ice cream buckets, with snap-down lids. The buckets were then stacked into polyethylene tote boxes (available from most department and hardware stores), and the units stored in a cool (45°F to 50°F), dry place, as recommended by the USDA.

Beans are one of the best choices as a survival food, not just for their longevity, but because they're higher in proteins than red meat. A two-pound bag of pinto beans yields about twenty-four servings of ½ cup (after cooking). A cooked bean serving of 1½ cups satisfies the minimum daily requirement of 2,000 calories.

Most cooks recommend soaking dried beans in water overnight before boiling them. However, there seems to be no difference in the end product if dried beans are boiled until tender, except for a longer cooking time. Experience has also shown that dried beans can be cooked quickly, in about ninety minutes, in a pressure cooker (even a covered cookpot with a rock on its lid), a little longer if left uncovered.

Rice

Rice has been a staple in my own wilderness kit for more than forty years. Like beans and barley, it's one of the original dehydrated foods, and is as lightweight as any of the more modern freeze-dried, packaged foods. Rice, raisins, and sugar, maybe a little cinnamon, was a traditional backwoods breakfast around many a campfire when I was kid.

Purpose-made hiking foods tend to be a little pricey, but you can save money by packing dried foods from home, like beans, rice, oatmeal, and macaroni and cheese. Make sure to repackage them to make them backpack-friendly.

Another beauty of rice is that it is not only good to eat by itself, but it goes with almost every type of food. Mixed with wild berries, apples, or any fruit, it becomes a dessert. Blend it with meat, fish, or poultry, add a few wild or domestic vegetables, and you have a hearty, stick-to-your-ribs dinner.

Pasta

This concoction of dried wheat is less amenable to long-term storage, but it has remained edible, even in a backpack, for up to three years. The trick is to protect it completely from moisture, because pasta can become mold-covered within a week. Yet, macaroni and spaghetti are sold packed in cardboard boxes that offer less protection than tissue paper. If sizes permit, boxes of macaroni and cheese can be repackaged, box and all, in a ziplock plastic bag, with a silica pack thrown in for good measure. (I save all of the silica packets that come in any other type of packaging.)

Salt

This critical component of outdoor-type foods is often overlooked, because the modern human gets far too much of it in his or her diet. But necessary it is, as evidenced by the real value that was placed on it in ancient times, when salt was actually a form of currency.

Actual needs vary with perspiration, exertion, and climate, but sodium deficiency manifests itself as cognitive difficulty (fuzzy thinking), blurred vision, cardiac arrhythmia (heart flutters), and a number of other ailments that often reveal themselves at the onset as a craving for salt.

At least as important is iodine, which is critical for thyroid health, especially for children and pregnant or nursing women. Iodine is fairly abundant in seafood, less so in dairy products, and more or less in vegetables and grains. About 70 percent of American households use iodized salt to meet the 150 microgram (mcg) daily requirement for an average adult—pregnant women need about 50 percent more, nursing mothers about 100 percent more.

Definitely include salt in your survival food stores. Salt intake does not, by itself, cause hypertension—that's why few doctors restrict salt intake of patients with high blood pressure these days. It does cause a body to retain fluids, which can raise blood pressure; if you suffer from diagnosed hypertension, it might be a good idea to have a sphygmomanometer (blood pressure cuff) on hand—disaster scenario or not. Several long-lived, battery-operated digital models are available inexpensively from most pharmacies.

Although humans in society tend to get too much of it, a hot-weather hiker who's sweating gallons on the trail can easily run low on this critical electrolyte.

FORAGING ON THE TRAIL

Wild plants are generally the most dependable food source. The majority of nutrients necessary to sustain human life can be obtained from plants alone, but as the Native Americans and mountain men of old were painfully aware, meat is also important in a balanced diet. Most plants are edible in terms of toxicity, but some of those that are considered edible are neither palatable nor digestible. And some of those that are very nutritious and digestible also taste terrible. This section will cover only those plants that are easily recognized, widespread, nutritious, and tolerable to the human taste buds.

Plants that have a short growing season, are limited to specific areas, or require boiling in several changes of water to remove their toxins won't be mentioned here. Mushrooms will be entirely ignored because they contribute little in the way of nutrition, are sometimes difficult to recognize, and certain species are downright lethal. The wild vegetables covered in this book represent only a small fraction of all edible wild plants. For those who want to include a more comprehensive catalog of wild plants in their survival kit, I recommend the Reader's Digest book *North American Wildlife* and *Edible Wild Plants* by Oliver Perry Medsger.

Burdock

Common burdock (*Arctium minus*) is a plant familiar to most of us; only Alaska and the extreme northern territories of Canada are beyond the range of this hardy weed. A thornless

Nearly all parts of burdock are edible: starchy taproot, tender young leaves, stems, and basal leafstalks that can be peeled and eaten raw or boiled. In bloom from July to October, it is found all over the North American continent. Burdock looks very much like rhubarb before flowering.

relative of thistles, burdock grows to a height of five feet and is common to fields, abandoned lots, open woods, and streambanks throughout its range. Immature plants very much resemble a hairy form of rhubarb plant, and the purple-tufted burs of the mature growth can be seen rising above the surrounding grasses in open fields.

The leaves, stems, and root of the burdock plant are all edible, but only the root is actually palatable. Some survival authorities have claimed that the fleshy stems can be peeled and boiled or eaten raw, but my own experience is that even with the bitter rind removed, the taste is sufficient to cause an involuntary grimace. The young leaves are also said to be good as a potherb (flavoring boiled food), but these too are very bitter. The large rootstock is exceptionally palatable, although in autumn it might need to be peeled and boiled, and this is the part best suited as a survival food. Were it not for the burdock plant's large size and great abundance, I would overlook it entirely.

Broad-Leafed Cattail

Cattails are nature's own smorgasbord, and no survivalist need ever go hungry where these distinctive plants grow. Both the common cattail (*Typha latifolia*) and its slightly smaller relative, the narrowleaf cattail (*Typha angustifolia*) are an excellent source of wild food every month of the year. The tall, reed-like growth form of the cattail is familiar to most folks. They can be found growing in ditches, marshes, along streambanks, and almost anywhere else fresh water is found in North America.

The edible parts of the cattail plant are the root, the core of the young shoots, the immature green seed head, and the thick yellow pollen from the spike atop the mature brown seed head. Young shoots begin to sprout in early spring, sometimes pushing their way upward through unmelted snow. These can be snapped off just below the surface of the ground and the white core eaten raw after the stringy green leaves have been stripped away, or they can be boiled briefly to make a dish known as "Russian asparagus." The raw shoots are crispy and pleasant to eat, with a flavor that I can only describe as a cross between celery and water chestnuts.

The thick rootstocks of the cattail can be eaten either raw or boiled any time of the year. Some authorities have likened them to potatoes, but the similarity is limited to the fact that both contain starch. In spring, young cattail roots are tender and crisp, but by autumn roots have developed a tough outer "bark" and a fibrous texture that bears little resemblance to the soft, fleshy potato with which we're all familiar. They are nutritious and palatable nonetheless, although some may find the very high starch content mildly objectionable.

The green cigar-shaped seed head was also eaten by the American Indians, who roasted or boiled them and then ate the cooked fruits like corn-on-the-cob. I've eaten these cooked either way and am not overly fond of the taste, which is slightly bitter, or the texture. The flesh is reportedly nutritious and digestible.

From May to July the male cattail plants produce large pollen-bearing spikes that sit atop the mature seed head. As a survival food, this pollen is both nutritious and very palatable. Large amounts of it can be gathered in a relatively short time by using a stick to knock the powder into a bush hat, canteen cup, or similar container. When enough of the powder has been collected, it can be mixed with a little water, stirred into a thick batter, and made into "pollen cookies" by spreading the mixture thinly over a hot rock or mess tin.

Common Plantain

Most obvious and plentiful of all nature's wild edibles is a weed known as common plantain (*Plantago major*) that grows from

Almost everyone in the world is familiar with the broadleaf cattail (*Typha latifolia*), which grows almost everywhere there's fresh water.

In spring, before the cigar-shaped seedpods develop, the white rootstocks of the broadleaf or common cattail are tender and crisp, but should be thoroughly washed or cooked before eating to eliminate possible parasites.

almost every patch of dirt, and even from cracks in concrete. This bane of gardeners and suburbanites across the United States was actually brought to North America from Europe to serve as a fast-growing vegetable half a millennium ago, and it has since established itself virtually everywhere. Able to thrive in the poorest soil, and in almost any climate, plantain is also one of the fastest growing ground plants; a mature plant that is cut off at the roots will begin to replace itself with a whorl of new leaves in about forty-eight hours.

One of nature's most useful plants—including for very nutritious meals, as a medicinal poultice for bites and stings, and even as a remedy for constipation—every hiker should be familiar with common plantain.

Nutritionally, plantain is equally amazing. Closely related to spinach, plantain leaves are even richer in vitamins A and C as well as iron. When the plant matures, the stalk-like seed pods that rise from its center are loaded with B vitamins. Taken as a whole, plantain is an almost complete multivitamin, including simple plant sugars (glucose and sucrose), proteins, and fiber. Some authorities have suggested that eating the seed pods will also bolster the body's natural insect-repellant skin oils with B12, which is distasteful to biting bugs.

Plantains may be eaten uncooked, but adult leaves tend to be a little stringy, and seed pods are a bit tough. Preparation is as simple as boiling washed plants until tender, then serving the leaves as you would spinach, or the seed pods as you might green beans or asparagus. A little apple cider vinegar helps to liven up the taste of cooked leaves, and I personally like them served hot with butter, salt, and pepper. Seed pods are good in stews and soups, stir-fries, or with melted cheese over them.

The value of plantain isn't limited to its culinary uses. An old and proven effective medicinal use of the crushed leaves is as a poultice bandaged directly onto bee and scorpion stings, spider and centipede bites, and infected lacerations. Modern medicine has not yet identified how a poultice of plantain leaves draws out venom and infection, but the plant has been a useful home-brewed first aid remedy for many generations. People who take dietary fiber might not realize that the psyllium husk in their supplements is from the same genus *Plantago*.

Maybe best of all, common plantain is not only hardy enough to sprout up from cracks in asphalt and concrete, even gravel roadsides, but it can tolerate a wide variety of climates. Plantains can be found in open places from Alaska through Mexico, from swamps to semiarid deserts. All of these qualities taken together make common plantain one of the first wild plants a survivor should learn to recognize and use.

Wild Carrot

Queen Anne's lace (*Daucus carota*) is the most common member of the wild carrot family. Its tall stems, with their frilly white umbels (many-lobed flowerheads), can be seen in every open field, pasture, and abandoned lot on the continent from May through October. The vertical leaves are frilly and even a bit scraggly, and the center of the umbel is dotted with a single, dark-colored flower. WARNING: There is some danger of confusing this plant with the very similar, very toxic poison hemlock (*Conium maculatum*), but positive identification can be made simply by smelling the root. Queen Anne's lace and its relatives have a strong odor of carrots; water hemlock does not.

Watercress

Watercress (*Nasturtium officinale*) is the survivalist's best, and sometimes only, source of fresh greens in the winter. It grows in running fresh water almost everywhere in the world, and when snow covers the ground it will be the only green plant found in streams, rivers, and springs. In summer it can be found growing in thick green carpets that sometimes completely choke smaller streams. The small clusters of tiny four-petaled flowers bloom from March to November, rising vertically from the surface of the water on slender stalks and ranging in color from white to light pink.

Watercress has long been sold commercially as a low-calorie, vitamin-rich vegetable. Eaten raw, it has a tangy, pungent taste faintly reminiscent of horseradish. Its vine-like growth form is browsed by freshwater snails that spread uncomfortable, sometimes incurable diseases (but always temporary, after about two months of intermittent misery), so it should be boiled before eating, or at least washed very thoroughly.

Reindeer Moss

Reindeer moss (*Cladonia rangiferina*) is an easily recognizable member of the lichen family common to the northern United States, Alaska, and nearly all of Canada. Reindeer moss is only one of many species

Found in open meadows and fields, Queen Anne's lace grows up to five feet tall with white umbrella flowers. Its edible white taproot smells strongly of carrots. It is very similar to the highly toxic hemlock plant, except that hemlocks lack the distinctive carrot odor.

Watercress's vine-like growth forms up to ten feet long, with small, white four-petal flowers from March to November. Its leaves are dark, shiny green and divided into many leaflets. Watercress may be found in nearly any fresh water and stream at all times of the year, sometimes growing so densely as to resemble a solid mass.

of lichen (hybrid plants that are half algae, half fungus) found throughout the world. Most of these are not only edible after boiling but contain nearly 100 percent of the nutrition required to keep a human alive and healthy in the wilderness. Many a stranded woodsman or explorer has survived a prolonged stay in the wilderness by eating these lowly plants. Reindeer moss is not at all tasty, but its many other qualities rate it as one of the best natural survival foods in the world.

Reindeer moss is found in open areas in mainly colder regions all over the world. A type of lichen (part plant, part fungus), it is crunchy, flammable when dry, and easily made into flour.

Reindeer moss prefers sandy, rocky open meadows and fields where it grows in carpet-like masses of dull blue, green, or gray that may extend for several yards in all directions. Individual plants range from two to four inches high. During dry weather these carpets will be brittle and crunchy underfoot, changing quickly to a spongy mass in the lightest rain.

Reindeer moss and other lichens should always be cooked before eating, because many of them contain a potent laxative that's nullified by boiling or baking. Other ingredients that are not destroyed by cooking include a high sugar content, numerous vitamins, many minerals, and a broad-spectrum antibiotic similar to penicillin.

Alaskans and Canadians living north of the Arctic Circle are reported to make a stimulating tea by boiling a strong concentration of crushed reindeer moss in water. I've tried this tea and judged it to be anything but stimulating, certainly not a favored beverage.

Reindeer moss can be prepared as a food by simply boiling it for a few minutes and then eating it right out of the canteen cup (awful), but the most common method of preparation is to boil it, mash it into a paste, blend it with berries, and bake it into cakes on a hot rock.

Violets

Violets (genus *viola*) are an abundant, nutritious, and very palatable wild vegetable that should never be overlooked by anyone facing a survival situation in warm weather, or just looking for fresh, wild vegetables with which to add variety to trail fare. There are more than sixty species

There are several species of violet, all of them edible, even palatable, growing in rich damp soil; this spring-blooming blue violet is among the most common, and the best-tasting.

growing in North America. Some have violet flowers, some white, some yellow, and at least one species is pink. Regardless of the color of the flower, all species are edible, although the downy yellow violet may cause a mild case of diarrhea if eaten raw.

Wild Leeks, or Ramps (*Allium atroviolaceum*)

This member of the family Liliaceae represents a very broad group of bulbed wild vegetables that are found across North America, and, indeed, around the globe. The family includes other better known species, such as sweet onions, chives, and garlic, and the much larger domesticated leek found on supermarket produce shelves. All share the pungent taste and odor that distinguishes onions among other vegetables. Preferred habitats are generally damp deciduous (leafed tree) forests with damp, black soil.

The eastern-growing broad-leaf species has been selected for this chapter, but its most common characteristics—anticholesterol, antihypertension, and general cleansing properties—are shared, more or less, by all leeks. The paired green leaves are of eastern leeks, along with their unmistakable smell of onion (often detectable even before you see the plants themselves), make them easy to identify.

Leeks and their kin are among nature's most nutritious wild vegetables, but their common pungent taste and odor (before and after eating) doesn't suit everyone's palate. The small-bulbed leek has always been a favored trail snack for northerners, and even those who aren't fond of leeks might enjoy a bit of added onion flavor to freeze-dried meals. The entire plant is edible, although its veined leaves are tough and best served cooked.

Perhaps best of all, juices from a leek's crushed leaves can be smeared onto the skin to repel mosquitoes, blackflies, and all biting insects. The downside is that the odor also repels people.

Spring leek is not just a bad pun, but a good way to remember when the plant is best harvested for food. This example's root bulb is a very strong onion.

7

HIKING MEDICINE

MEDICAL TRAIL HAZARDS

Note: For her assistance in composing this chapter, I would like to acknowledge the valuable assistance of Ms. Cheanne Chellis, a paramedic of more than thirty years who possesses advanced certifications for cardiac, pediatric, and wilderness first aid. In her career, she has saved so many lives, before victims ever reached a hospital, that it seemed almost irresponsible not to consult her for chapter 7 on medicine.

A first-aid kit can be a blessing on the hiking trail. With it, a wound warranting medical attention might be reduced to an inconvenience under conditions that didn't favor the weakened. It's very important to have, at minimum, a few of the most important first aid implements (for cuts, sprains, pain, allergies, and so on) at all times.

POISON IVY, POISON OAK, AND POISON SUMAC

If you've ever suffered an allergic reaction to any of these, then you don't need to be told how miserable the rash, itching, and in some cases, blisters caused by them can be. Since the three are so similar in how they're contracted, their symptoms, and treatment, we'll treat them as the same affliction, except where otherwise noted.

Many myths exist about how one can develop a case of poison ivy. In fact, contracting poison ivy, oak, or sumac is no more complicated than brushing bare skin against their leaves. Most of the time, potential victims simply didn't recognize or notice the plants. It pays to know what these plants look like at every stage of their lives, where they might be found growing, and to be on the lookout for them in likely habitats during their growing seasons.

To clarify, the poison ivy, oak, and sumac have a usually shiny oil called urushiol coating their leaves, and contact with this oil causes allergic reactions. It has been estimated that nine out of ten people are allergic to urushiol, depending on the pH balance of their skin.

You cannot "catch" a reaction, because oils are too heavy to be transported on the wind, except from the smoke of burning green plants (a fact that was discovered the hard way by groundskeepers). But if you walk through the plants and then take off your boots, urushiol oil will likely be rubbed off onto your hands, and then transferred to other parts of your body and even to other people. Clothing, pets, firewood—any surface which might have come in contact with leaves is a possible vector for contamination.

The effect of urushiol oil on susceptible skin is actually a chemical burn. In early stages, when the affliction is just a mild skin rash, diphenhydramine hydrochloride, a popular histamine-blocker better known by the brand name Benadryl, may cause symptoms to disappear entirely. But once it has advanced to the point of blistering or beyond, a victim's only recourse is to let it heal.

BEES AND WASPS

According to the Centers for Disease Control, in the period from 2000 to 2017, a total of 1,109 deaths from hornet, wasp, and bee stings occurred, for an average of 62 deaths per year. Deaths ranged from a low of 43 in 2001 to an all-time high of 89 in 2017. Approximately 80 percent of the deaths were among males. Be careful, boys.

Shown here in perhaps its most classic form, shiny oils covering the three leaves of a poison ivy plant cause chemical burns on the skin of anyone unlucky enough to have the correct pH balance; there is no cure except time and healing, but calamine lotion is most used to obtain relief from itching.

Beware this type of paper wasp nest (bald-faced hornets are shown); should you brush aside a sapling from which one is hanging, you and your companions will likely face the wrath of residents that are fiercely protective and can sting you as many times as they want.

Experience has shown that fleeing a disturbed bee or wasp nest is exactly the best defense. Bees and wasps don't carry grudges, but they will defend their nests vigorously. The quicker you get yourself beyond their defensive perimeter, the quicker the insects will return to guard duty of their nest. Put simply, run! And don't stop until the bees or wasps stop chasing you, which will generally be within one hundred yards. Once the tiny warriors are convinced that you no longer pose a threat to their nest, they'll stop attacking and return home.

A wasp or bee doesn't do damage with a "bite," as many people think. That misconception stems from a tendency for wasps to use their pincer-like jaws to anchor themselves to your skin while driving home their stinger. The bite does little or no harm, but the sting can have a serious effect on some folks.

To an average person in generally good health, bee stings aren't dangerous. Expect a localized swelling around the sting site (the uticaria), caused by an allergic reaction to venom injected as an insect stings. Experienced beekeepers, who have been stung many times, react to a sting with an "Ow," and that's the end

Not every animal fears wasps and bees; as shown here, bears, protected by fur too thick for insects to penetrate, regularly rip apart paper nests to lick-up the larvae they contain.

of it—no swelling, no more pain at all. But most of us haven't been stung enough to have developed an allergic immunity (in a few cases, numerous stings can cause a lifetime allergy). A sting, or worse, multiple stings, can cause a systemic reaction. That means that venom spreads from the sting site through the body, where it negatively affects a victim's respiratory system.

Should a companion be stung and react with difficulty breathing, even an hour or so after the fact, they need immediate, urgent treatment with a fast-acting antihistamine. A prefilled, one-time-use syringe containing a dose of the prescription-only drug epinephrine, known by the brand name EpiPen, is most ideal. Dosages are generally predetermined as 0.15 milligrams for youngsters (twelve years and under, weighing ninety pounds or less), and 0.30 milligrams for adults—be certain not to use an adult dose for a child, as the supercharging effects of epinephrine can cause permanent heart problems. Be aware that EpiPens are standard equipment for ambulances and the jump kits of wilderness paramedics.

Some hikers don't know they're allergic to something until it causes an allergic reaction. If you're miles away from a road, and an EpiPen isn't available, you need an acceptable alternative. The best answer is Benadryl, sold more inexpensively under its chemical name diphenhydramine hydrochloride (HCl). This powerful over-the-counter antihistamine, once sold by prescription only, has proven its potential to save lives by temporarily depressing the body's own, sometimes deadly, symptoms to an allergic reaction.

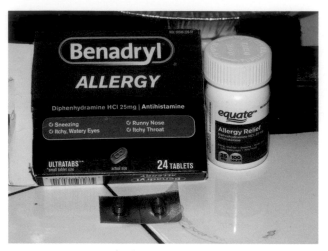

Diphenhydramine hydrochloride, better known by the brand name Benadryl, is a must-have component of every hiker's first-aid kit.

If sold in capsule form, the fastest way to get diphenhydramine into a victim's bloodstream is to break a capsule and pour its contents directly under the tongue, where it can be absorbed sublingually into the bloodstream. If in tablet form, it should be chewed-up before swallowing it down with water. The taste is just horrible, but the drug can save your life.

When using either epinephrine, diphenhydramine, or even nothing at all, lay a victim flat on their back, separated from the ground by a closed-cell sleeping mat (a hiking must-have) or a thick pad of dry forest duff (detritus on the forest floor) to prevent ground temperatures of less than 98.6°F from stealing body heat. Elevate the feet about 15 degrees above the head to ease strain on the heart, and cover at least the upper torso with a blanket or opened sleeping bag.

SNAKES

There exists an exaggerated and unmitigated fear of these legless vertebrates, perpetuated by children's tales and movies that never depict the animals as friendly, and especially not as the generally harmless animals they actually are.

Most species of snakes throughout the world are not venomous, although many more possess prey-holding serrated teeth that can draw blood if larger specimens are forced to bite in self-defense—which is the only reason that any snake bites. With the exception of, ironically, extremely venomous species like America's eastern diamondback (*Crotalus adamanteus*) of the coastal plain of the southeastern United States (Louisiana east along the coast through Florida, up to southern North Carolina), snakes will always try to flee at the first sign of a hiker's approach. "Bush" snakes, like the eastern diamondback and the fer-de-lance of the Amazon rainforest, take refuge under low-lying shady brush, often the sides of foot trails which they travel on for convenience. Most hikers walk right on past the alert but motionless snakes. Make a sudden move—like tripping on a tree root—and the snake may feel as if it's being attacked. This problem is made worse by a diamondback's rattle being muffled by undergrowth.

If you spy any coiled and rattling snake (be aware that many nonlethal snakes, like the robust hognose group, vibrate their tails in brush and hiss), the situation can be defused with a single step backward. The striking distance of even a large rattlesnake is under two feet, and you should bear in mind that any snake realizes its disadvantage against a foe fifty to one hundred times its own size.

Northern water snakes (*Nerodia sipedon*) inhabit half of the eastern United States. The species is marked similarly to the venomous cottonmouth, which it is often mistaken for, even as far north as Michigan, hundreds of miles north of the cottonmouth's range. Ironically, the nonvenomous northern water snake is even more aggressive than the cottonmouth, especially when massed together along shorelines during the spring mating season. Although the snake has rows of teeth that can draw blood, and sometimes grows to more than three feet in length, it is not venomous.

Despite the apparent violence of this scene, garter snakes like this one are entirely harmless to humans.

The real cottonmouth, or water moccasin (*Agkistrodon piscivorus*), is a venomous snake capable of delivering a potentially fatal bite. A species of pit viper in the subfamily Crotalinae of the family Viperidae, like rattlesnakes (cottonmouths have no rattles), it is the world's only aquatic viper, seldom found far from water. During spring and after heavy rains, when rivers are swollen, the snakes tend to migrate in clustered rafts, carried on the currents; it's during these times, when being crowded together increases tensions among the snakes, that they are most likely to bite any animal that comes into range. The species is native to the southeastern United States.

Many companies market knee-high lace-up snake boots, which are inconvenient, somewhat less than comfortable, and (in this author's opinion), totally unsuitable for long hikes. Snake boots are designed to address a phobia more than a need, but they've found a market among boot-buyers.

If it does bite, a snake understands that its victim will likely kill it in retaliation, thus ending any chance a snake can fulfill its most basic instinctual need, which is to procreate. For that reason, many vipers, asps, and cobras tend to simply lie quiet as hikers walk by, avoiding the chance of confrontation as they hide in nooks and crannies in which they feel safe. A walking stick, among its many other uses, is a good way of forcing hidden snakes, and other creatures, to reveal themselves while still at a safe distance.

Should one of your troop suffer a bite from a known venomous snake (remember, many biting serpents are not venomous), keep the bitten limb lower than the rest of the body to inhibit circulation of venom. Apply a snug—not tight—tourniquet above (nearer the torso) the bite area, and if a stream or lake is available, hang the bitten limb, at a lower level than the victim's body, in the colder water. Do not try to walk a victim out, as activity will help to speed the venom through the body. Any activity at all is discouraged; bite victims should lie quiet by a warm fire, insulated from the ground by a sleeping pad or pallet, and try to relax.

The most recommended treatment for a snakebite is to get the victim to a hospital as quickly as possible. There, an application of the proper antivenom is the best solution to venom injected by a given species of snake—it is never necessary to kill the snake, but it is a good idea to photograph it, so that experts can make positive identification.

SCORPIONS

On a trip to Colorado's Gunnison Gorge Wilderness Area, I had an unpleasant experience with a scorpion. After feeling a sudden stinging shock run through my right knee, my headlamp revealed the crushed body of a striped bark scorpion. In the morning, my knee was a bit stiff, but I was able to hike down the mountain with minimal pain, and I took ibuprofen for the swelling and discomfort.

Armed with hemotoxic and neurotoxic venom (like a cobra), the eastern diamondback is the most dangerous viper in North America. It prefers overgrown, jungle-like habitats in warm climates, where it can hide well camouflaged under ground cover at trailside and lie in wait for prey. Startling a sleeping eastern diamondback can be dangerous.

During the drive home, my right leg began to throb as it pushed against the gas pedal. When I stopped for fuel, I could barely stand while leaning on the open door, and I walked with a pronounced but still nominally painful limp. It was obvious, even under my loose-fitting military-style cargo pants, that my right, scorpion-stung knee was almost twice the size of its opposite.

Back home, the inflammation slowly disappeared over the next few days, and there was never more than tolerable pain and stiffness. No trip to my doctor was necessary, nor was there a need for anything but over-the-counter medication for swelling.

As it turns out, my experience was actually more severe than most. Most scorpion sting victims recover in just a few hours and experience less inflammation and pain. There are indeed more venomous, more dangerous species within the same family of arachnids, like the Arizona bark scorpion, whose range overlaps the less dangerous striped bark scorpion that stung me. It pays to know what potentially harmful animals inhabit the area you'll be hiking, and insects and arachnids are usually at the top of that list.

SPIDERS

Spiders are another creature that has historically been unjustly maligned. Not that there aren't species that can be lethally dangerous, like the funnel web spider of Australia, or the legendary black widow. But if you're a typical person, the number of spider bites you'll suffer in your life will range from zero to the number of socks on your feet.

Like snakes, spiders don't live to bite humans, and if you want to avoid an arachnid's fangs, it's usually not difficult—just a few precautions. Knock down spiderwebs that cross your path with a hiking staff before walking through. Whenever you remove your boots, turn them upside down and smack them with your palm to dislodge spiders (and scorpions). Shake out blankets, sleeping bags, and beach towels before using or packing them away.

All spiders are venomous, because injecting venom through their hollow fangs is how they immobilize prey that is, in many cases, larger and stronger than they are. If you or a companion should be bitten, and the bite area becomes more than a localized redness with localized pain or if the pain begins radiating beyond the site, the negative symptoms can be lessened by taking two diphenhydramine (Benadryl) tablets.

Tissue-dissolving effects of the venom cannot be halted. Initially there will be a hard, raised bump, followed several days to several weeks later by a usually concave depression in the skin. Eventually, the depression may heal to look normal again, but in some cases, especially bites from the brown recluse, or violin spider (*Loxosceles reclusa*), doctors have described the healed bite as looking "as if a scoop of flesh had been removed," even if the victim did not suffer a systemic allergic reaction. Personal experiences with bites from large wolf spiders have been similar.

Black Widow Spider (genus *Latrodectus*)

Most dangerous spider bites in the United States are from the southern black widow (*Latrodectus mactans*), the western black widow (*Latrodectus hesperus*), and the often beautifully colored northern black widow (*Latrodectus variolus*). Black widow spiders are found throughout North America, but are most common in the southern and western

All spiders are venomous, because that's how they get food. However, many (including the infamous brown recluse) lack the jaw strength to drive their fangs into human skin without counter-pressure from above. This member of the wolf spider family can bite, and it is relatively venomous, but its bite is seldom more than a painful inconvenience.

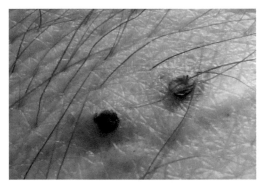

This is a typical bite from a large Wolf Spider.

areas of the United States. They are identified by the pattern of red coloration on the underside of their abdomen, sometimes with striped or splotched topsides, depending on species. They are often found in workplaces containing undisturbed areas such as woodpiles, the underside of eaves, fences, and other areas where debris has accumulated.

Like many spider species, black widow spiders build webs between objects to ensnare flying insects, and bites can occur when humans come into direct contact with these webs. Every seasoned hiker has walked through fresh spider webs strung across a trail (black bears, who consider arachnids a delicacy, actually look for them). Spiders whose webs are broken in this way stand a good chance of landing on a hiker's person, and female spiders, the only gender big and strong enough to penetrate human skin, can become uncharacteristically aggressive when guarding their egg sacs. Spiderwebs that stretch across your trail should be knocked down with a stick. If a hiking staff is used, make certain that a web's resident doesn't cling to the stick or hang from it by a web strand.

A typical southern black widow with her egg sac, which she will defend aggressively.

Black widows are perhaps most infamous for residing in outdoor toilets, where they lie in wait for carrion flies and houseflies, frequently on the underside of toilet seats. Most black widow bites have happened in this manner, and those bites tend to be more serious because they're inflicted in a place with maximal blood flow. Chemical toilets have helped to reduce the attraction outhouses have for flies and spiders, but the problem has not yet been eliminated.

A time-honored safety precaution has been to lift and then let drop a toilet seat before sitting, to dislodge any spiders that might be hanging from its underside and to help frighten off any that might be around it. Always practice what soldiers call situational awareness—inspecting floors, walls, ceilings, and especially corners—to ensure that arachnids aren't watching you.

All spider bites are distinguished by paired side-by-side puncture marks in a victim's skin. The black widow's venom contains both a hemotoxin (flesh dissolver) and a neurotoxin that produces pain at the bite area and then, in more acute allergic reactions, spreads to the chest, abdomen, or the entire body. In extreme cases, cardiac arrest can occur, sometimes accompanied by respiratory failure, and possibly even death. Two Benadryl tablets help to alleviate both symptoms. (Information courtesy of US CDC.)

Brown Recluse Spider (*Loxosceles reclusa*)

The brown recluse spider, also known as the violin spider for the markings on its abdomen, is most commonly found in the midwestern and southern states of the United States. It is brown in color with a characteristic dark violin-shaped marking on its head and has six equal-sized eyes (most spiders have eight eyes). Brown recluse spiders are usually found in workplaces with secluded, dry, sheltered areas such as underneath structures and logs or in piles of rocks or leaves. If a brown recluse spider wanders indoors, it may be found in dark closets, shoes, or attics.

This subspecies of brown recluse spider (*Loxosceles reclusa*) is a classic "fiddleback" spider, from the violin-like marking on its thorax and abdomen.

The brown recluse spider lacks the jaw strength to bite humans without some form of counter pressure. For example, if a human rolls onto it, the unintentional contact can trap the spider against the skin (spiders of all types tend to avoid skin contact with humans). Most bites occur in bed, when a recluse, true to its name, seeks out darkened hiding places. Bites may cause a stinging sensation with sometimes intense localized pain. A small white blister usually develops at the site of the bite. The venom of a brown recluse can, and usually does, cause a severe lesion by destroying skin tissue (skin necrosis). This skin lesion will require professional medical attention. (Information courtesy of US CDC.)

HYPOTHERMIA

The hazards of hypothermia cannot be overstated. Few people today are unlucky enough to be exposed to the elements for an extended period, but campers, hikers, and anglers who may find themselves separated from shelter and warmth by more than a few hours are smart to guard themselves against cold, regardless of latitude.

The term "freeze to death" is a misnomer; any air temperature below the normal 98.6°F human body temperature is robbing you of warmth, and without an insulating shield the rate of heat loss can be life threatening in temperatures as high as 50°F. Lower the temperature of the strongest man's internal organs by just 5°F, and he will be incapacitated—maybe comatose—and headed toward certain death unless his body is rewarmed immediately.

But it isn't cold alone that poses a need for protection; at a relatively balmy 35°F, the cooling effect on a body exposed to winds of 25 miles per hour is the same as it would be at an ambient temperature of only 8°F. Couple that with a soaking rain that alone can lower felt temps by 20°F in a windless environment, and the combination can be lethal. Among professional survival instructors, no weather is more dreaded than 40°F with a hard rain.

In Canada and Michigan's Upper Peninsula, there are no warm rains, and grizzled old-timers will tell you that a cold autumn rain is more life threatening than a subzero blizzard.

Other warm-blooded creatures are spared our vulnerability to cold because they possess oily fur or feathers that stop wind, repel rain, and retain body heat while blocking ultraviolet rays from reaching the skin. None can dissipate heat as well as our naked, perspiring skin, but even a mouse is far better equipped to tolerate cold than an unclothed human. To survive in all but the warmest climates we need a facsimile of a fur coat.

Not all garments are suitable for outdoor use, and that includes clothing made from cotton, or any blend of cotton. The problem with cotton is its ability to absorb and hold several times its own weight in moisture, the same characteristic that makes it such a good choice for towels and washcloths. When dry, cotton fabric retains enough warmed air between its fibers to be a good insulator, but any moisture it contacts will be absorbed, displacing critical air and compressing fibers into a soggy mass. Worse, cotton dries very slowly, subjecting its wearer to constant and prolonged cooling that dissipates a large amount of body heat. The cooling effect is such that a hypothermia victim dressed in wet cotton will actually be warmer when stripped to his bare skin.

Wool remains the standard garment material for cold weather use; its naturally oily fibers shed rain and absorb very little moisture, insuring that a layer of warm air remains trapped between the elements and a wearer's skin. On the downside, wool is infamous for being itchy against bare skin, and old-style knit wool socks are notoriously abrasive to perspiring feet.

The modern answer to wool is fabric woven from plastic fibers. Marketed with names like nylon, X-Static, Capilene, and Polartec, these synthetics are kind to bare skin, nonabsorbent, and provide a good friction-free layer between feet and footwear. Some fibers are hollow, some are blended with strands of silver to reflect warmth back toward the skin, but all repel water from the outside and quickly dissipate perspiration from inside to keep wearers drier and warmer.

Hikers wearing a combination of a synthetic base layer covered by heavier wool or synthetic midlayers, both covered by a lightweight wind- and waterproof shell layer, have the basis of an insulating system that can handle any climate on Earth. In cool weather, or during periods of heavy exertion, the windproof shell can be removed to allow perspiration and excess heat to escape. In warmer weather, a good base layer alone helps to maintain a constant body temperature, even in light rain, by mixing and matching clothing layers to changes in temperature and humidity. A fanny- or daypack is recommended for day hikes.

Be forewarned that not all hypothermia is obvious. Trekkers in the outdoors can experience what seasoned survival instructors know as creeping hypothermia. The patient doesn't shiver or complain of cold. However, he or she might stumble over words, mutter unintelligibly, and fail to comprehend or execute even simple instructions. The most frightening aspect of creeping hypothermia is that victims demonstrate no clear signs of being cold until they just die, usually in their sleep.

The remedy for hypothermia, whether its symptoms are obvious or not, is to rewarm a victim's core. That is, to elevate internal organ temperatures back to a normal level. Never massage a hypothermia victim's limbs or extremities. Doing so will injure already damaged skin and muscle tissue, and actually make the problem worse by drawing warmed blood away from the core, where it's most desperately needed by the heart, lungs, and kidneys. And never, ever rub snow onto cold hands or feet—never. In fact, ignore the limbs and extremities altogether until a victim's body temperature is back to normal. A hypo-

A cold rain is by far the most dangerous weather a hiker can face, especially in terms of hypothermia, and particularly if it's windy.

thermia victim who complains of extreme pain in toes and fingers (it's a myth that severe hypothermia is painless; the process is excruciating) is actually recovering.

The proper treatment is to get a victim out of wet clothing. Expect them to resist, because most mistakenly believe that to lose even wet clothing is to lose warmth. Then, get warm (not hot) liquids into their bellies. Water is arguably best, but I personally recommend the stimulant effect of caffeine. Ignore the body's exterior until a victim starts to actively complain about cold fingers or feet. Remember, you do not want to draw warmed blood away from internal organs before they've been warmed, regardless of how cold extremities might be.

When mental faculties and motor control have been restored, only then should you warm up the rest of the victim's body. The naked-body-to-naked-body rewarming technique under a blanket or inside a sleeping bag is overrated and mostly myth. I recommend a warmed car or a campfire, for medical and legal reasons.

HYPOGLYCEMIA

It was the fifth morning of an eight-day backpacking excursion into Mackinac State Forest at the northwestern tip of Michigan's mitt, and it had been raining hard since our arrival on March twenty-sixth. Not a gently falling rain, but a hard, cold downpour that pounded through leafless tree branches to hit the naked forest floor with a sound like hard-sizzling bacon. And it never stopped, not even for a moment.

My fourteen-year-old nephew, Josh, and I were in the middle of a week-long backpacking trip, and we'd banked our fire from the night before with three large dead logs. When we rolled them over, placing the heat-dried, unburned sides directly against the coal bed, they burst into flames. By adding small, then progressively larger wet twigs and branches, we soon had a crackling blaze. Josh was standing with his back to the fire, where rising heat waves actually pushed falling raindrops away from its perimeter, creating a dry warm spot in the midst of constant deluge. But while the side facing the fire warmed and dried, the outward side got wet and cold.

While waiting for coffee water to heat, Josh's eyes suddenly rolled back into his head to show white, and he simply collapsed. I watched in horror as he sat down heavily, directly on top of the bed of orange hot coals that lined our firepit. As if in slow motion, I saw his right hand, clad only in a fleece overglove and knit liner, drive into those coals until it was embedded to the wrist into a place hot enough to melt copper. Miraculously, there wasn't so much as a red spot anywhere on the young man. Even his outer clothing wasn't burned, saturated as it was under rain that fell faster than it could run off, and the overlap between jacket and glove cuffs had kept his wrists from touching live embers.

The cause of this near disaster was hypoglycemia, or more specifically a body's normal reaction to having available energy in the form of blood-borne sugars depleted by the increased demand of keeping warm. When blood sugars are gone, the body is designed to switch over to using fat reserves as energy, but the first several times hypoglycemia occurs can literally come as a shock. Panicked by loss of readily available fuel, the brain can react by shutting down systems needed to power the body. Symptoms range from nausea, tunnel vision, and overpowering fatigue to outright loss of consciousness. Long distance runners call it "hitting the wall," and anyone who participates in heart-pumping activities that demand stamina, from mountain biking to cross-country skiing, and especially snowshoeing, can expect to experience hypoglycemia.

The cure in every instance is as simple as increasing a victim's blood sugar to normal operating levels. In Josh's case, it was a cup of hot cocoa for quick energy and warmth, followed by a starchy, slow burning breakfast of rice and raisins. He was back to normal after about ten minutes but had little memory of falling into the fire.

Conventional survival wisdom places feeding oneself low on the list of priorities for staying alive in a wilderness environment, based on a belief that it takes about three months for a typical human to die of starvation. In reality, the greatest danger is likely to be more immediate, stemming from symptoms of hypoglycemia and the loss of function they cause. Slipping off a rocky or icy trail is one of the more serious secondary hazards of reduced efficiency from having low blood sugar. Falling into a blazing fire is right up there, too.

From helping to keep you warm during an unplanned night in the woods to helping you to feel more positive and energized, having a pocketful of snacks rich in sugars, fats, and proteins can make a real difference in how much fun you have on any wilderness excursion. Quickly absorbed sugars and fats from chocolate are great for cutting off hypoglycemia at the first signs. Slower burning carbohydrates from cheese, peanut butter, and dried fruit act like slow-burning hardwood in the metabolic furnace. Summer sausage can provide both proteins and fats. All of these will fit into jacket pockets. For all-day hikes, a comfortable daypack laden with under ten pounds of snacks, an extra shirt and socks, and a few light luxuries can keep adventures from becoming hardships.

Whether hiking, scouting hunting territory for a coming deer season, or just exploring new places, remember that traversing wild country on foot can consume more than twice the

Some of the quickly metabolized, long-burning trail foods dumped out from an experienced day hiker's pack.

energy burned in normal life. The unpleasant symptoms of hypoglycemia should be expected and guarded against by everyone who walks in the woods.

DEHYDRATION

Dehydration does not happen without plenty of warning signs. The first and most obvious warning, usually noticeable by a victim, is that urine becomes stronger-smelling, and its color turns darker. Bright yellow is a sure sign that you need to "push" water, drinking until you can't comfortably drink any more.

Never deprive yourself or companions of drinking water. Water should never be rationed, or you'll run the risk of medical complications that are far worse than being thirsty. There are good reasons for sweating and peeing, and you should never deny your biological machine the cleansing and lubrication that it needs to operate efficiently. I won't even use deodorant that has antiperspirant in it.

The best place to store water is in your belly, and the only solution to running out of drinking water is to find more. Presuming an air temperature of 70°F and a moderate-level hiking trail, it's prudent to estimate daily hydration needs at two gallons per person per day. No one wants to carry extra weight, but too much water is far preferable to running out.

For some desert hikes, it may be prudent to establish water caches along the way. It's surprising that this hasn't become a standard practice whenever possible, as it used to be. Recyclable food-grade polyethylene terephthalate (PET) bottles are commonly used for juices, soda, and other consumables, and these bottles are often sturdily made. The bottles have proved resistant to rodent teeth, difficult to damage, and, maybe best of all, free. I've personally stored tap water in PET bottles for eighteen years, with no loss of potability, no leakage, and no absorption of taste. Stashing two or three gallons under a rock cairn midway along a brutal desert trail can double, even triple the range of a hike, and at virtually no cost.

JOINT INJURIES

Joint injuries, especially to the ankles, have become almost synonymous with hiking. Uneven terrain, exposed tree roots, stones that roll underfoot, rain-slick logs and timbers, vines—any of these can conspire to suddenly shift your weight uncontrollably in a direction and to an extent that your joints were not designed to bend. A bone intersection that is hyperextended beyond its limits can stretch the ligaments that hold joint bones together, and pull, even tear, tendons that connect muscles to bones.

Because prudent hikers have, since the beginning of time, carried extra weight in the form of tools and other necessities, most joint and bone injuries happen to the lower, weight-bearing portions of the body. Sprained ankles are by far most common, and almost entirely preventable by wearing the proper footwear—tied-on in the proper way. As mentioned earlier in chapter 1, any trail that is not a paved sidewalk demands ankle-high, dedicated hiking boots, preferably bound using the around-the-ankle woodsman's tie (see page 5). The slightly modified sneakers known as cross-trainers are entirely unsuitable for hiking, if for no other reason than their total lack of ankle support.

Hikers, especially those who've suffered past joint injuries, can take some precautions. Previously injured joints tend to "roll," or temporarily pop out of place. This painful problem can be protected against by binding the joint across its middle and at least six inches above and below with an elastic bandage or tape, even over a hiking boot. Better-fitting alternatives are products like the Copper Fit support sleeves, endorsed by, among others, NFL players. Different products protect and support all major joints, including lumbar (small of the back) support belts that seem custom made for anyone who carries a backpack.

Ice is the recommended treatment for twisted joints, but ice is seldom available unless a troop is also packing a cooler of beverages. Instead, cool streams have proved very effective for soaking turned ankles and other injured joints to alleviate swelling and pain. The soothing effects of a running stream are helpful for muscle strain and whole body weariness, too. The length of time that a damaged limb or body should soak is subjective; soak the affected part in cool running water until you feel good enough to carry on. And do not try to tough it out; nature laughs at tough guys and gals.

Ibuprofen, known by the brand name Motrin, is both a potent pain reliever and an anti-inflammatory, just the ticket for an overworked and overstrained hiker. Never exceed the recommended dosage, as ibuprofen can cause gastrointestinal erosion, and always take it with plenty of water. Don't use ibuprofen as a crutch to enable you to walk or otherwise over-use an injured joint or muscle, as this can prompt you to injure it even more severely.

FRACTURES

In the case of an actual broken ankle, it's best not to move a victim at all. Moving them, or trying to splint a broken bone, can cause more damage. According to our consulting paramedic and wilderness first aid expert, the best method of treating an obvious break or, worse, an open break (also called a compound fracture), is to use a "soft splint." First cover any open wounds with a sterile dressing to keep out dirt and debris, then roll a closed-cell foam pad around the damaged limb and tape or tie the ends to keep it rolled. A closed-cell foam pad is stiff enough to keep a leg immobilized and soft enough to protect it.

This Splint, Aerospace, Medical (SAM) bone and joint immobilizer is an inexpensive item that should be in every hiker's first-aid kit; a roll 4.24 inches wide by 3 feet long averages about ten dollars per item.

For arm fractures and breaks, a SAM Splint, a bendable, laminated aluminum–foam splint almost seems made for the hiker. Available in thirty-six-by-four-inch rolls that weigh less than five ounces, these padded splints can be cut to fit the job—or bone, as the case may be. After the desired length has been removed, bending it lengthwise into a trough shape creates a stiff channel that can be conformed to cup, cushion, and brace an arm. After placing the stiffened channel so that it spans and supports both ends of a break, tape its ends to the affected limb with several wraps. Most SAM Splints have instructions printed right on them, making it easy to do it right.

Injuries to the bones and joints should mark the end of a journey for victims. Toughing it out should never be an option, because it's possible, even probable, that a simple, healable injury might become damaged enough to require surgery, and perhaps even reach a point where it cannot be repaired. A hiker should never willingly endure a discomfort that can be avoided. Nothing good comes of doing that, and you can sure make things worse.

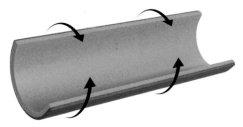

A section of SAM Splint bent into a stiff channel that can immobilize a fractured bone or damaged joint.

LACERATIONS

Cuts and abrasions to the hands and fingers are the most common injuries in the woods, because many routine tasks involve using a sharp edge.

Originally developed for factory workers who handled sometimes sharp-edged parts, but didn't want the bulk of a full glove, finger tape has become an indispensable component of the savvy hiker's first-aid kit.

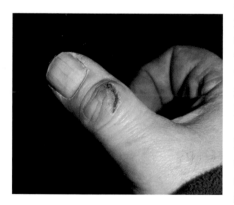

After a cut has healed sufficiently to close itself, looser wraps of safety tape over a fresh application of antibiotic ointment protects against painful bumps, allowing the cut to heal itself naturally.

First, always work to stop the bleeding. The wilderness is the wrong place to be leaking important body fluids. Next, clean and sterilize the wound so that infectious organisms are not trapped inside. Finally, close the severed edges of the wound, so they can heal back together.

A field-proven cut-kit consists of a tube of triple-antibiotic ointment, at least three pressure dressings, and several rolls of medical safety tape in various widths. Medical-grade cotton gauze safety tape is impregnated with natural latex, which causes it to stick tenaciously to itself, but nothing else, with a grip that holds even when wet.

After sterilizing the wound, wrap several loose (never tight) turns of tape around the finger on either side of the cut, gently pushing the edges almost together. Skin edges should be left slightly apart to permit fluids to drain as an injury heals from the inside first. If bleeding persists, add a pressure bandage, cut to a size that more than covers the wound, and snugly tape it directly on top of the wound to apply constant, localized downward pressure. After about eight hours, unwind the tape, clean the wound—which has usually stopped bleeding—and apply another, looser wrap of safety tape to protect the injury from contamination and bumps. Safety tape has a multitude of other uses, from splinting broken bones, wrapping sprained joints, and immobilizing neck injuries to reattaching a fishing pole's eye, mending a broken snowshoe frame, or wrapping a knife handle to give it a better grip.

The same procedure works with larger appendages, but a gash to the thigh, for example, should initially be closed by butterfly sutures. Essentially very sticky tape strips that are designed to stick tight to skin, butterfly sutures are meant to replace stitches for skin-closure applications, but they might not hold a wound closed unless the entire limb is immobilized for at least three days. Even then, do not exert the wounded area or limb more than is absolutely necessary, and immediately stop if you feel so much as a sting from the sutures, lest you tear the wound open again.

Never attempt to suture any wound with needle and thread. Sterile suture kits are available from medical supply outlets for about six dollars, but few of us have the medical training to reattach flesh, and gangrenous infections have resulted from sealing in infectious agents. Even large open wounds can eventually heal closed without sutures; the primary concern, after you stop the bleeding, is to prevent infection.

DIARRHEA

The young man got high marks for enthusiasm, but it quickly became clear that his intestinal condition should have dictated that he not come along on this backpacking trip. Not a half-hour passed that he wouldn't drop his pack and head for the bushes. Aside from health concerns, like dehydration sickness, his frequent stops were disrupting the timetable of his entire troop. The final analysis was that the stricken hiker had contracted the intestinal cyst *Cryptosporidium parvum*, probably on a previous trip, and now the low-grade fever and gastrointestinal problems that are typical of intestinal cyst infections were creating problems for everyone.

Diarrhea in general is caused by the lower intestine attempting to purge what it considers to be an irritant. Intestinal cysts anchor themselves securely until they mature and they (dead after procreating) and their eggs are expelled after about two months. Influenza-caused diarrhea is caused, or worsened, by inflammation of the digestive tract.

The bottom line is that curing the root cause of diarrhea is generally not possible, but there are numerous effective treatments to alleviate its most inconvenient symptoms. Everyone knows good old Pepto-Bismol, the wintergreen-flavored pink stuff that adults give to kids with upset stomachs. But the most effective belly-settling ingredient is often underfoot in the form of wintergreen plants, evergreen shrubs

An old home remedy for potentially embarrassing and always inconvenient diarrhea on the trail is a sweet-smelling tea made from the thinly shaved roots of the wild blackberry bush. Use roughly one root per cup water, boiled for at least five minutes.

with typically two succulent leaves whose flavor gives the plants their name. A tea (which becomes pink, like Pepto-Bismol) made from these leaves has long been a remedy for sour stomachs.

Better for diarrhea is loperamide hydrochloride, probably better known under the brand name Imodium AD. Available in individually sealed 2 milligram capsules, or as a liquid, these have a place in every hiker's first-aid kit.

On trail, an old do-it-yourself remedy that has worked well for centuries is a sweet tea made from shaved blackberry roots. This old woodsman can't explain how it works, I can only say that, based on personal experience, it sure seems to.

CONSTIPATION

Constipation is an equally distasteful topic. The malady is real, though, and it can quickly morph into a potentially lethal intestinal blockage.

Ideally, a hiker, or anyone really, should experience at least one constructive bowel movement per day. It isn't unusual for some hikers to feel so uncomfortable without the bathroom facilities they're used to that they sometimes become anal retentive. The reluctance to leave the most obvious of sign in the wild dates back to an instinctive insecurity over revealing oneself to potential predators.

The biggest cause of constipation is dehydration. Like any machine, the human body requires lubrication to keep running smoothly. Deny it the required moisture it needs to operate, and the body will develop sticking points, so to speak, that can range from kidney infections to chronic headaches.

In some cases, including personal experience (which many editors hate that I mention), hikers have had to use a finger to dislodge hard balls of fecal matter that were stuck in their colons. As distasteful as this is to address, being the victim is worse, because by the time a person reaches the decision to manually clean their colon, they're in considerable discomfort. And the operation itself is less than pleasant (or sanitary), too.

As with every problem, the best answer is to avoid becoming dehydrated in the first place. Drink plenty of fluids, even if it's coffee or flavored water, although plain water is recommended. How much water a person needs is subjective, dependent on air temperature, exertion levels, individual metabolism, and so on, but urine should be almost clear.

Keeping well hydrated is especially important if you'll be eating dehydrated or freeze-dried foods. One young fellow caused himself extreme discomfort by

This eight-pack of twenty-ounce bottles of electrolyte-replenishing sports drink is not out of place in the bottom of a hiker's pack, and when empty, the individual bottles might prove too valuable in themselves as you pack out your empties.

consuming the fruit bars from two military MREs as if they were candy. And this author once did the same by attempting to live on granola bars during a three-day backpacking trip. Based on vicarious and personal experiences, this is a lesson best learned from a book.

BITING BUGS 101

If you find your best fishing holes and camping spots in the backcountry, you've noted the more or less limited effectiveness of insect repellents there. Brand doesn't matter when blackflies, mosquitoes, deerflies, horseflies, and stable flies are driven by the smell of warm blood to assault a body.

Commercial repellents help, but the truth is that when newly hatched bugs rise up in black clouds, bloodsuckers just don't respond to odorous chemicals. The oil in some repellents provides a mechanical protection, like the bear grease once used by northern American Indian tribes, because bugs don't tolerate sticking to their victim's skin. But the instinct for females to ingest the blood proteins they need to lay fertile eggs often proves stronger than repellents in the deep woods.

The most prized item in my own biting-bug defense arsenal is a head-size tube of no-see-um netting sewn shut at one end to form a bag. With the mesh bag pulled over your head and the open end draped loosely over the shoulders, you'll have a see-through shield that physically blocks attacking bugs from reaching your face or getting into your collar. I still sew my own tube nets from no-see-um netting, but you can find these effective bug (and sunlight) shields at sporting goods stores for around ten dollars.

When insects are swarming, only a fine-mesh head net keeps the mosquitoes from flying into this person's eyes and facial orifices, permitting him to at least function in some discomfort.

Long sleeves and pants are required during bug season, and visitors to the woods should at least have those clothing items with them. Some outdoor trousers convert to shorts with zip-off legs that carry conveniently in their own cargo pockets.

Clothing may be pretreated with repellent sprays containing pyrethrin (natural) or permethrin (synthetic), the stuff found in pet flea sprays. Both chemicals are mildly toxic to humans, and should not be applied directly to skin, but fabric treated with them becomes poisonous on contact to all species of biting bugs, including ticks and chiggers. Clothing treated with either chemical, available in sprays at outfitter and pet supply stores, remains toxic to insects for several days, and retains some repellant qualities even after a hard rain.

Almost ubiquitous in some form along riverbanks, yarrow is frilly-leafed with flat umbels made from concentrations of small four-petaled flowers (not always white) blooming in late summer. The pungently scented yarrows are one of nature's most potent insect repellents, and every hiker should commit this plant to memory.

Tansies, once used as funeral flowers because their pungent scent helped to conceal the scent of unembalmed bodies, are common to moist, dark soil across North America, and their juices can also serve as effective insect repellents.

Several easily recognizable and usually abundant plants offer some protection from flying hordes of biting insects. Common yarrow, tansies, oxeye daisies, and other members of the aster or daisy family may be found almost everywhere mosquitoes and blackflies hatch, and all of them contain pyrethrin in their juices. Rubbing crushed leaves and flowerheads onto clothing provides effective protection, and rubbing "yarrow juice" into my dog's fur has long been a good deterrent of deer and horseflies and ticks.

Tansies and yarrows are common to moist areas across North America. Although mildly toxic to humans, small quantities are sometimes used in salads or as a black pepper substitute. Their best known use was as a funeral herb, where they helped to mask the odor of decay while keeping flies from crawling over the deceased, and began the tradition of having odorous flowers at funerals. Hunters may appreciate that the tansy's strong odor is a naturally occurring scent that won't spook animals.

Catnip is another naturally occurring plant with insect repellent qualities. Fond of open, mostly shaded places, catnip is widespread across North America, where it has been used for centuries as a stimulating tea. The oils contained in its leaves are responsible for inducing the euphoric behavior demonstrated by housecats that eat them, and these oils are poisonous to most insects. Juices from the crushed leaves can be safely rubbed onto skin and clothing to afford protection against mosquitoes, but blackflies and deerflies seem mostly immune.

Smoke is one of the best insect repellents. A campfire kept purposely smoky with damp, half-rotted wood or wet leaves repels biting bugs of all types. In a past era it wasn't uncommon for woodsmen to employ a lighted cigarette or cigar to accomplish the same thing away from camp. Nowadays a less objectionable and more fragrant incense stick can provide the same protection from insects—but be very careful of sparks! During rest breaks and at camp a perimeter of lighted repellent incense sticks shoved upright into the earth will throw off enough smoke to deter bloodsucking critters.

A simple plastic bag and your own hands is one of the most effective methods for pressing small quantities of juice from green plants.

TICKS

Ticks are easily the most feared of bloodsucking bugs. Tick-borne diseases, particularly Lyme disease (*Borrelia burgdorferi*), are becoming more frequent. Reported cases in the United States rose from twelve thousand in 1995 to thirty-six thousand in 2016, according to the CDC. As most cases go unreported, the CDC believes the true number of infections is likely ten times that number. At present, the FDA has licensed no vaccines to aid in the prevention of Lyme disease.

Not all ticks carry the disease, but might instead carry a host of other diseases, like anaplasmosis or *Anaplasma phagocytophilum*. Lyme-infected ticks may attach to any part of the

This female American dog tick is one of the most feared animals on the continent.

It is widely believed that a blood-filled tick is one the ugliest (and concerning) life forms on Earth.

body, but prefer migrating to moist or hairy areas such as the groin, armpits, and scalp. Almost everyone is susceptible to tick bites, but campers, hikers, and even gardeners are at greater risk. As suburbs expand into previously wooded areas, deer, squirrel, and mice populations in those places thrive, because human residents tend to run off their predators. Increased feeding opportunities for ticks (and fleas and mites) also increases their populations.

For Lyme disease to be transmitted, a tick needs to feed on the host for twenty-four hours. In most cases, tick bites occur in the summer months, but tick bites can also happen in the warmer months of autumn, too, and throughout winter where temperatures remain warm.

LYME DISEASE: SYMPTOMS AND STAGES

Symptoms of early-stage Lyme disease include:
- muscle and joint aches
- headache
- fever
- chills
- fatigue
- swollen lymph nodes

A more common symptom of Lyme disease is a rash called *erythema migrans*. Eighty percent of bite victims develop a rash, often with a bull's-eye appearance.

(continued on next page)

Later-stage symptoms may take weeks or months to occur, and include:
- heart-rhythm irregularities
- arthritis (mostly in large joints, especially the knee)
- nervous system damage

If you believe you have Lyme disease, a doctor can confirm or disprove the suspicion with a blood test. But be mindful that the Lyme bacterium will not be detectable until your own body begins to develop antibodies to fight it, which generally takes two to five weeks. If your doctor also suspects Lyme disease, they may begin you on a regimen of antibiotics, just to be safe. Permanent damage to joints and nervous system usually accompanies late Lyme disease, but it is seldom fatal.

Precautions Against Tick Bites:
- Stay on trails, if possible; avoid brushy and tall grass, especially in midsummer.
- Wear light-colored clothing that contrasts with darker-colored ticks.
- Wear long pants, long-sleeved shirts, and boots or socks with sandals.
- Tuck pant legs into socks; tuck shirt into waistband.
- Wear a hat.
- Spray at least 15 percent DEET on clothes and exposed skin, especially wrists and ankles.
- Walk in the center of trails.
- Wash and dry clothing after being outdoors.
- Do a careful, mutual check with a buddy after outdoor activities.

HOW TO SAFELY REMOVE A TICK:
1. Using fine-tipped tweezers, grasp the tick as close to the skin's surface as possible.
2. Pull upward with steady, even pressure. Don't twist or jerk the tick. Your goal is to remove the entire tick, ideally in one piece, including the mouth parts embedded under the skin. If you are unable to remove the mouth easily with clean tweezers, leave it alone and let the skin heal.
3. Thoroughly clean the bite area and your hands with rubbing alcohol, an iodine scrub, or soap and water.
4. Never crush a tick with your fingers. Dispose of a live tick by putting it in alcohol, placing it in a sealed bag/container, wrapping it tightly in tape, or flushing it down the toilet. For more information on the safe removal, disposal and identification of ticks visit CDC.gov/ticks.

It's important that you remove ticks from your skin immediately, safely, and thoroughly, as this days-old tick removed from a pet dog illustrates.

PARAMEDIC-APPROVED FIRST-AID KIT

Being human means being fragile. We like to think of ourselves as tough, but the truth is that it's pretty easy to incapacitate a human being. An injury that ruptures or severs an artery can bleed us to death in four minutes. A hard knock to the brainpan can cause fatal cerebral hemorrhaging. There are more ways to kill a human than there are to flay the proverbial cat.

The odds of surviving a potentially fatal trauma have risen drastically in the past few years. Advances in medical science have given people without formal medical training a better understanding of human physiology and spawned a host of potentially lifesaving tools that couldn't have existed for our predecessors even a generation ago.

(continued on next page)

The "golden hour," the first sixty minutes after a victim is injured that medical experts agree are most critical to a victim's survival, has grown generally longer as more efficient, more portable lifesaving tools come to the fore.

Every hiker ponders such things in the woods, especially when there's no cell reception and medical help is a half-day away at best foot speed. But even in a city, with an ambulance available in just minutes, prompt first aid treatment can save lives. To help me address that concern, I turned to the experts in first aid, the paramedics of Allied Ambulance. Thanks to their guidance, here's the first-aid kit you'll find in my backpack today:

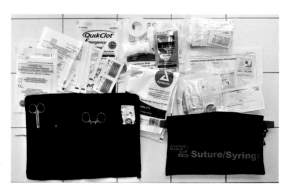

A comprehensive first-aid kit can save your life, and the lives of others.

- 1 bottle ibuprofen, 50 count
- 1 4x4 gauze sponge
- 1 large roll gauze
- 1 roll one-inch-wide self-adhering tape
- 1 elastic wrap
- 1 sterile suture kit (installed with a drain tube)
- 1 chewable Pepcid AC heartburn tablet
- 2 alcohol prep pads
- 2 QuikClot antihemorrhagic sponges
- 6 sealed diphenhydramine HCl (Benadryl) capsules
- 6 loperamide HCl (Imodium A-D) antidiarrheal capsules
- 1 triple antibiotic ointment, tube or envelope
- 1 miniature LED headlamp
- 1 penlight
- 1 toenail clipper
- 1 tweezer
- 1 bandage scissor
- 1 small magnifying glass
- 1 first aid manual

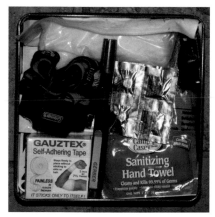

Fitted into a discarded candy tin, this paramedic-built first-aid kit is more effective than any of its manufactured counterparts.

SIGNALING FOR HELP!

A person stuck in a wilderness survival dilemma generally has two choices: either make his or her own way back to civilization as efficiently and intelligently as possible, or stay put and hope that someone will come looking to take him or her back home. Which strategy is best depends on the situation, on a victim's fitness to travel, and the tools at hand. The uninjured survivor of a "soft" plane crash in the Canadian Rockies in late summer might be smart to hike through the mountain passes shown on his map before they become choked by deep snow. The same survivor would be foolish to try that in late autumn, when he would likely be caught in the middle of a blizzard.

If a situation demands staying put, you will probably welcome help from outside, especially if medical problems are part of the equation. In view of the overwhelming job faced by search and rescue (SAR) personnel—and the budget constraints of these often poorly funded agencies—it behooves anyone who can envision the possibility of needing rescue to be trained and equipped to get that message across effectively.

The Signal of Threes

Everyone in need of rescue should know the "signal of threes," because it is simple, and likely to be recognized as a call for help by search and rescue personnel around the world. For hunters, three rifle shots into the air have been a call for help since repeating arms were invented. The same principle applies to almost anything that can be used to create an abrupt, noticeable sight or sound: two stones clacked together from the side of an echoing canyon; three flashes from a bright flashlight or headlights; three loud whistles or blasts from a horn; or three hard whacks of a stout pole against a tree trunk (this may also bring Sasquatch seekers, maybe even a Sasquatch, I'm told).

Sending a signal of threes means having someone close enough to see or hear it, so try to match signal to terrain. Flashes from the brightest torch or flashlight are difficult for a pilot to see through heavy forest canopy, and a signal mirror might not work at all—both of these are best sent from high, open places that are visible from many miles. Audible signals can be more versatile,

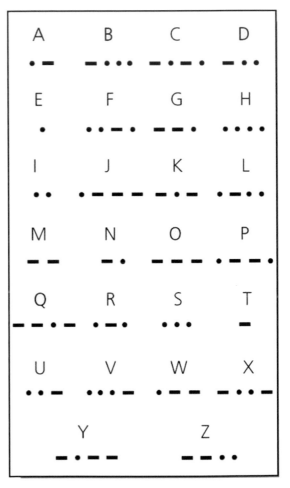

While everyone should memorize how to signal SOS, Morse code can convey many different messages.

because they cannot be blocked from sight, but they too should be generated from open country—if sound echoes there, it's probably a good spot.

More noticeable, if not recognizable, are the Morse code letters SOS that has become synonymous with any plea for help. The letter S consists of three dots (• • •), which translates into three short signals. The letter O is three dashes (— — —), or three long signals. To send an SOS with a flashlight, for example, the person signaling would flash the beam with three short bursts (S), followed by three bursts of longer duration (O), and finally three more short bursts (S). The SOS signal can also be made with sounds, as with a whistle. With rocks knocked together or "tree clubbing," signals in which the audible part is uncontrollably brief, dashes and dots are spaced as pauses between sounds, not the sounds themselves.

Signal Mirrors

In open country, where you can get a clear shot at directing a beam of reflected sunlight onto a distant target where someone might notice the flash, a signal mirror can be a lifesaver. Best of these are the molded Lexan polycarbonate types, with star-shaped sighting holes and the ability to float on water (about twelve dollars in sporting goods stores). With the sun facing you, look with one eye through the mirror's sighting hole, then place the target in the center of the sighting hole (this may be difficult if the target is a moving airplane). Tip the mirror one way, then the other, keeping your target fixed in the sighting hole, until a bright spot appears in its center.

This floating Lexan signal mirror makes it easy to focus the sun's concentrated light on distant objects.

Place that bright spot onto the target, and reflected sunlight is being directed onto that spot. Move the spot onto and off the target to send flash signals.

Ground-to-Air Signals

The ability to signal overflying aircraft may be vital. The simplest method is to keep a fire burning brightly through the night, then to keep the hot coals producing smoke during daylight hours by fueling them with wet, half-rotted wood. The threat of forest fires makes pilots alert for smoke and flame. Ideally, a fire should be sited where it can be seen both from the air and from the surrounding terrain, but in heavily canopied forest or jungle, dense smoke may be the only means of sending a call for help to the outside.

Other ground-to-air signals have included stamping-out the letters SOS in snow, using debris on an open beach, or shaped with logs in a clearing. Better are the internationally recognized emergency ground-to-air signals shown here, formed the same ways, but with a more extensive vocabulary to transmit specific, urgent needs—like medical assistance. They can be created from rocks, rotting logs, vegetation—any medium that lends itself to forming the desired symbols, and which contrasts as markedly as possible with the surrounding terrain.

International Emergency Ground-to-Air Signals

Which Way? | This Way | OK to Land | I'm OK

No | Yes | I Don't Understand | I Need a Compass

I'm Hurt | I Need Medical Assistance | I Can't Proceed | I Need Food and Water

Forming these symbols on the ground so that they can be seen by overflying aircraft tells a pilot what your situation might be. The author has had to use the "LL" symbol for "I'm okay" several times to keep small planes from buzzing his camp.

Personal Locator Beacons

Personal locator beacons (PLBs) are battery-operated one-way transmitters that send signals at frequencies monitored by search and rescue receivers. A fallen mountain climber who trips his or her PLB sends a unique distress signal to an overhead satellite, which relays the signal to a mission control on Earth. Each PLB transmits a digital ID that is registered to its owner, and GPS-equipped models can bring rescuers to within feet of the beacon, which is especially valuable to victims of snow or mud slides. A traceable signal enables SAR paramedics to arrive on scene without having to search for the victim and armed with insulin or other drugs that might be specific to that victim but are not normally carried.

PLBs are registered to NOAA (www.beaconregistration.noaa.gov) at no charge, but bear in mind that some states pass along the very significant cost of a rescue in an invoice to the rescued party. Unit prices begin at around three hundred dollars for basic 406 MHz models, and about five hundred dollars if you want one equipped with GPS. Designed to be worn around the neck, battery life is functional—up to forty hours—and units are waterproof, usually to three meters. One drawback is that, like satellite telephones, the signal can be affected and even blocked by terrain and overhead canopy, so units should be triggered from open terrain (preferably where a helicopter can land).

Flares

Signal flares are a tried-and-true method of attracting attention, but only if those who might notice a flare are within sight. Probably most recognizable are the classic orange break-action single-shot pistols commonly seen in plane crash movies. Available in 25mm or 12-gauge calibers, usually with an attached bandolier of four extra cartridges, these plastic guns can launch a 16,000 candlepower "meteor" flare to about four hundred feet, with a burn time of about seven seconds.

Several other types and sizes of aerial flares are available, usually with cylinder-shape tube launchers, some reusable, and in a variety of colors. Marine flares include parachute types that can stay aloft for more than half a minute, and even flares that are designed to burn out before landing, to minimize the danger of a forest fire. Nonlaunched road-type flares can be useful for sending a bright signal from high or otherwise open ground, but they have also proved most likely to start fires.

Many outdoorsmen do not carry flares, and in spite of its life-saving potential, an aerial flare is not always useful. Mountain climbers should not make an ascent without "pencil" flares, no bush or island-hopper plane is airworthy without an extensive survival kit that includes pistol and flares, and every canoe or kayak should have some type of aerial flares on board. Conversely, a canoeist or backpacker under the thick canopy of an Ontario forest might be better off trading the weight and bulk of a flare kit for something that will prove more useful in a close environment.

Finally, always file an itinerary of your intended travel route, even for short hikes in wilderness areas that you know well—those who come looking for you might not be equally familiar with local geography.

If having a unit is within your budget, a personal locator beacon like this is almost a guarantee that you'll be rescued if you get into trouble.

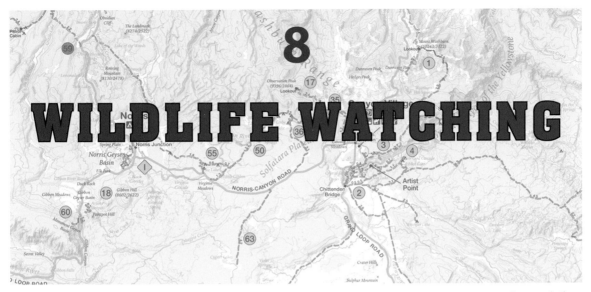

8

WILDLIFE WATCHING

Seeing animals in their native habitat is one of the most important reasons that a hiker shoulders a backpack, whatever its size, and heads into the wilderness for one or more days. Seeing a moose foraging at the water's edge is a vision that will never leave you.

Even better is having developed the tracking and stalking skills to locate and to photograph, as proof of your claims to others, a bear or wolf in its own habitat. The attraction of competitive games to modern humans is that they trigger a hunting instinct that evolution has determined we would find pleasurable. Finding pleasure in the act of hunting can now be expressed through wildlife watching and photography.

BINOCULARS

Whether watching wildlife or a football game, almost every outdoor activity can be enhanced by binoculars. Like other predators, humans have eyes paired at the fronts of our heads so that twin images of the same scene, viewed from slightly different angles, can be compared by the brain sixty times each second. This three-dimensional dual-imaging system gives us the power to discriminate precisely between objects at different ranges, resulting in unmatched distance and depth perception.

Unlike a monocular or riflescope, a binocular utilizes our stereoscopic ability to estimate distance, but enlarges objects from as low as four times for "stadium" binos to twenty-five times for stargazing models.

A binocular is a necessary part of every hiker's kit, because they, in effect, give you supervision, even at night. Carry as good a pair as you can afford.

Increasing magnification requires more ambient light to illuminate the ocular (eyepiece) lens, so lower magnifications are best in dim light. Larger objective lenses gather more light, but at the expense of portability.

Helping to resolve that dilemma is the metallic lens coating developed by Carl Zeiss prior to WWII. By applying the principle of a two-way mirror, Zeiss found he could prevent light penetrating the objective lens from reflecting back out, thereby brightening what a viewer sees at the ocular lens. Today's coatings also act as light filters, blocking darker UV rays while absorbing brighter infrared hues, thus enabling a small objective lens to deliver the same brightness as a larger uncoated lens. Even at night, a good binocular will let you see more clearly than you could with a naked eye.

Objective lens diameter and magnification also affect "field of view" (FOV), the real diameter of the circular area visible through them at one thousand yards (or meters in some models). The higher the magnification, the narrower the FOV. The larger the objective lenses, the greater the field of view. Hockey fans and birdwatchers who follow fast-moving objects lean toward wide-view 4x to 8x models. Lower magnifications also require less ambient light, making them better in shadowed forests or concert halls.

There are essentially two types of binocular. Traditional Porro prism types are the bulkiest, with ocular and objective lenses offset to accommodate large prisms in the viewing barrels. This configuration is preferred by boaters for whom size and weight are less important than maximum clarity. Hunters and birdwatchers want maximum viewing quality with minimum bulk, so most opt for a more streamlined roof prism binocular. Roof prisms provide virtually the same optical quality as Porro prisms, but with prisms contained inside straight, more compact viewing barrels.

Look for the designation BaK-4 in the description of a binocular's prisms. BaK-4 refers to a barium-crown glass prism with the best visual fidelity available. To see which prism is inside, hold the binos about six inches in front of your eyes and look through the ocular lenses; a BaK-4 prism will reveal itself a perfect circle, while the lesser BaK-7 borosilicate glass prism shows as a fuzzy-edged square.

Birds aren't the only sights that a great pair of binos can reveal to hikers who might not otherwise see them.

Not all binoculars are built to endure prolonged exposure to wet or cold, and if moisture gets inside, internal lens surfaces may remain fogged indefinitely. Waterproof binoculars with sealed nitrogen-filled tubes will have that feature printed on their bodies.

Always try out a binocular before purchasing, even if you have to do it inside the store. None of us has the same face, and you want to be able to use the binocular comfortably. Pull-out eyecups that accommodate eyeglasses and sunglasses are a plus, and the distance between ocular lenses (interpupillary distance) should adjust to fit your eyes comfortably. A good test is to bring the focused bino to your eyes quickly; you should immediately see a clear, bright picture through them, without squinting.

How well a binocular performs is linked to its price, because precision lens coatings and sealed construction add cost to the manufacturing process. A blister-packaged department store bino that retails for thirty dollars can't provide the optical quality of a higher-end model with more features. Among birdwatchers, a group that knows its binoculars, the consensus is that field-worthy binoculars have no more than 10x magnification (any more is hard to hold steady), objective lens diameters of at least 32mm, and a starting price of two hundred dollars.

Larger objective lenses take in more available light and, thanks to precision metallic glass coatings, amplify that light enough to see in darkness better than the naked eye.

Whatever its cost, treat your bino like a valuable optical instrument. Most important is preserving its lens coatings. Treat these coatings gently; keep lenses covered when not in use, and use only soft, clean cloths to wipe them. Never use saliva to clean any coated lens, because enzymes in saliva are corrosive to them and can degrade optical performance.

CAMERAS

Thanks to digital cameras, everyone can be a skilled photographer. And thanks to cellular telephones, virtually everyone has a digital camera. Comedians have pointed out how mobile telephones have, in a single generation, become as integral to daily human attire as curly tails are to Siberian huskies.

The cameras that have become a part of every cell phone are pretty good—good enough to compile a visual database of interesting points that you can take home and keep forever. It is not unheard of for hikers and campers to make discoveries about nature, wildlife, and animal migrations that had escaped the notice of paid professional biologists and botanists. A camera helps you to present indisputable proof of those discoveries.

Cell-phone cameras have reached the point of being quite good, but professional photographers still rely on dedicated cameras to capture a maximum of reproductive quality from a scene.

The most important secret to getting great photos of memorable sights is to be there.

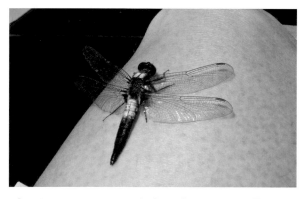

There are so many sights that you will want to capture and keep from every outing that a digital camera is sure to become a must-have item in every backpack.

More common is a desire to simply take home tangible memories; photos are reminders of what may be one of the best experiences in a lifetime. A moose or bear is always photo worthy, but watching a darning needle dragonfly emerge from its underwater cocoon and climb to the top of a reed to dry its beautiful metallic blue or green body before flying away is truly a sight to behold.

As a baseline, four megapixels (a simple measure of camera quality, more megapixels being better) is adequate for your needs, and most cell phones easily meet that requirement. But as you get more serious about photography and want higher-resolution (better) photos of subjects that are farther away, you might want to move up to a dedicated camera that does nothing except take photos.

Photographing wildlife is one of the most challenging and frustrating exercises that any of us will ever attempt, as you'll doubtless discover for yourself at some point. Animals and birds do not tend to be photogenic; they flit, fidget, flutter, hide, and often flee at the first sight or scent of a human being. And if there's more than one person present, these reactions may increase exponentially. Therefore, you must be prepared.

You will want to capture and preserve sights like this one.

RECOGNIZING WHAT YOU SEE: A SHORT COURSE IN TRACKING AND READING SIGN

Despite a supernatural aura that surrounds the activity, tracking terrestrial creatures is only as complicated as learning to recognize disturbances caused by an animal's passing and then translating that "sign" into a coherent picture. The skills are very much like those used in forensic science, where an investigator pieces together clues and assembles them to arrive at a conclusion about what probably occurred there. Tracking is like putting together a puzzle, and the experience is so enjoyable that it's a wonder more people don't do it just for fun.

Deciphering paw and hoof impressions is fundamental to tracking, and a seasoned tracker can glean considerable information from a single print. Size indicates an animal's age up to adulthood, and depth in mud or snow yields an estimate of weight. Excepting that female mammals are typically smaller than males, gender cannot be determined from a track, but it might be made evident by other behaviors.

Front and hind tracks are usually easy to differentiate, because forefeet are noticeably larger in most species, particularly fast runners. Reasons include a barrel chest that permits lungs to expand to great volume but makes its owner front heavy. Forefeet, which hit the ground first at a running gait, require a larger surface area for traction and to increase weight distribution (flotation) on snow and other soft surfaces.

Four-legged animals walk primarily on the outer edges of their soles, which increases the distance between contact points (straddle) and provides greater stability. This configuration—opposite our own—means the innermost toe or hoof is smaller and prints more lightly than the largest outermost toe.

A colloquialism for alertness is to "be on your toes." Its stems from the way animals designed for fast running walk "digitigrade" fashion, with body weight always leaned forward to

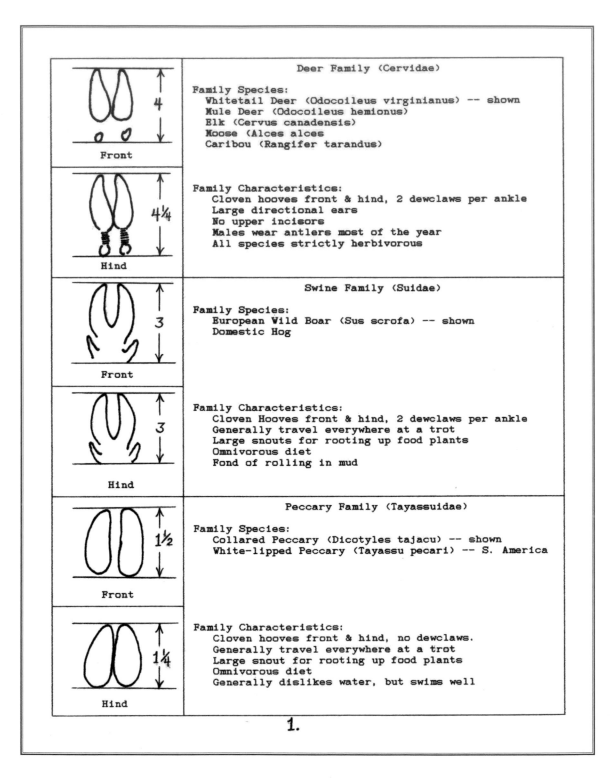

Deer Family (Cervidae)

Family Species:
    Whitetail Deer (Odocoileus virginianus) -- shown
    Mule Deer (Odocoileus hemionus)
    Elk (Cervus canadensis)
    Moose (Alces alces)
    Caribou (Rangifer tarandus)

Family Characteristics:
    Cloven hooves front & hind, 2 dewclaws per ankle
    Large directional ears
    No upper incisors
    Males wear antlers most of the year
    All species strictly herbivorous

Swine Family (Suidae)

Family Species:
    European Wild Boar (Sus scrofa) -- shown
    Domestic Hog

Family Characteristics:
    Cloven Hooves front & hind, 2 dewclaws per ankle
    Generally travel everywhere at a trot
    Large snouts for rooting up food plants
    Omnivorous diet
    Fond of rolling in mud

Peccary Family (Tayassuidae)

Family Species:
    Collared Peccary (Dicotyles tajacu) -- shown
    White-lipped Peccary (Tayassu pecari) -- S. America

Family Characteristics:
    Cloven hooves front & hind, no dewclaws.
    Generally travel everywhere at a trot
    Large snout for rooting up food plants
    Omnivorous diet
    Generally dislikes water, but swims well

Front — 4
Hind — 4¼
Front — 3
Hind — 3
Front — 1½
Hind — 1¼

1.

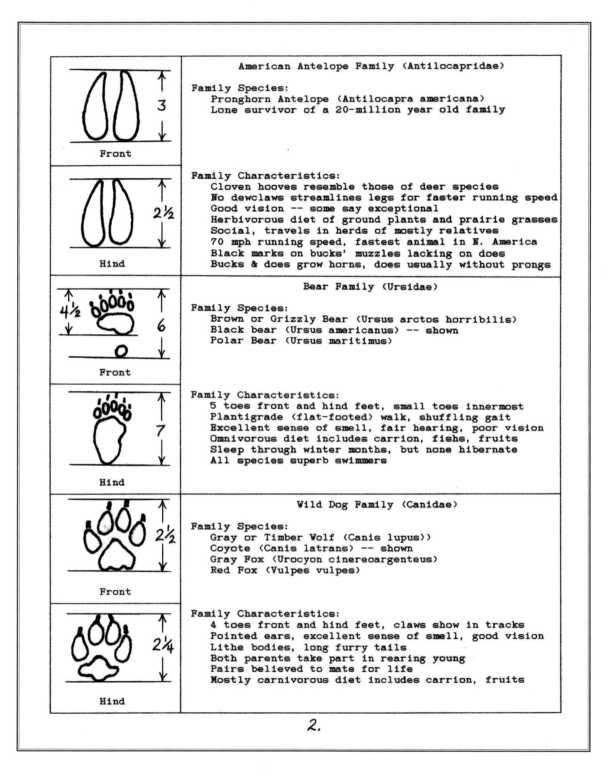

	American Antelope Family (Antilocapridae)
Front — 3	**Family Species:** Pronghorn Antelope (Antilocapra americana) Lone survivor of a 20-million year old family
Hind — 2½	**Family Characteristics:** Cloven hooves resemble those of deer species No dewclaws streamlines legs for faster running speed Good vision -- some say exceptional Herbivorous diet of ground plants and prairie grasses Social, travels in herds of mostly relatives 70 mph running speed, fastest animal in N. America Black marks on bucks' muzzles lacking on does Bucks & does grow horns, does usually without prongs
	Bear Family (Ursidae)
Front — 4½ / 6	**Family Species:** Brown or Grizzly Bear (Ursus arctos horribilis) Black bear (Ursus americanus) -- shown Polar Bear (Ursus maritimus)
Hind — 7	**Family Characteristics:** 5 toes front and hind feet, small toes innermost Plantigrade (flat-footed) walk, shuffling gait Excellent sense of smell, fair hearing, poor vision Omnivorous diet includes carrion, fishs, fruits Sleep through winter months, but none hibernate All species superb swimmers
	Wild Dog Family (Canidae)
Front — 2½	**Family Species:** Gray or Timber Wolf (Canis lupus)) Coyote (Canis latrans) -- shown Gray Fox (Urocyon cinereoargenteus) Red Fox (Vulpes vulpes)
Hind — 2¼	**Family Characteristics:** 4 toes front and hind feet, claws show in tracks Pointed ears, excellent sense of smell, good vision Lithe bodies, long furry tails Both parents take part in rearing young Pairs believed to mate for life Mostly carnivorous diet includes carrion, fruits

2.

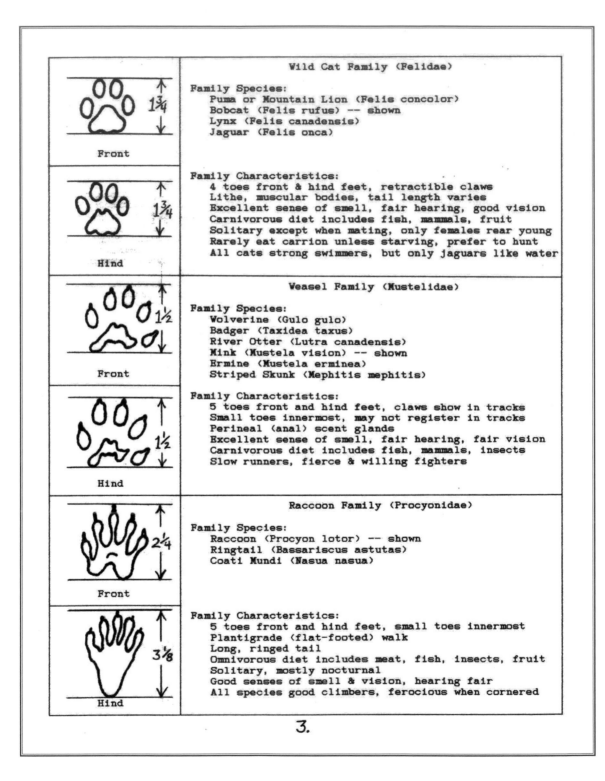

Wild Cat Family (Felidae)

Family Species:
    Puma or Mountain Lion (Felis concolor)
    Bobcat (Felis rufus) -- shown
    Lynx (Felis canadensis)
    Jaguar (Felis onca)

Family Characteristics:
    4 toes front & hind feet, retractible claws
    Lithe, muscular bodies, tail length varies
    Excellent sense of smell, fair hearing, good vision
    Carnivorous diet includes fish, mammals, fruit
    Solitary except when mating, only females rear young
    Rarely eat carrion unless starving, prefer to hunt
    All cats strong swimmers, but only jaguars like water

Front — $1\frac{3}{4}$
Hind — $1\frac{3}{4}$

Weasel Family (Mustelidae)

Family Species:
    Wolverine (Gulo gulo)
    Badger (Taxidea taxus)
    River Otter (Lutra canadensis)
    Mink (Mustela vision) -- shown
    Ermine (Mustela erminea)
    Striped Skunk (Mephitis mephitis)

Family Characteristics:
    5 toes front and hind feet, claws show in tracks
    Small toes innermost, may not register in tracks
    Perineal (anal) scent glands
    Excellent sense of smell, fair hearing, fair vision
    Carnivorous diet includes fish, mammals, insects
    Slow runners, fierce & willing fighters

Front — $1\frac{1}{2}$
Hind — $1\frac{1}{2}$

Raccoon Family (Procyonidae)

Family Species:
    Raccoon (Procyon lotor) -- shown
    Ringtail (Bassariscus astutas)
    Coati Mundi (Nasua nasua)

Family Characteristics:
    5 toes front and hind feet, small toes innermost
    Plantigrade (flat-footed) walk
    Long, ringed tail
    Omnivorous diet includes meat, fish, insects, fruit
    Solitary, mostly nocturnal
    Good senses of smell & vision, hearing fair
    All species good climbers, ferocious when cornered

Front — $2\frac{1}{4}$
Hind — $3\frac{1}{8}$

3.

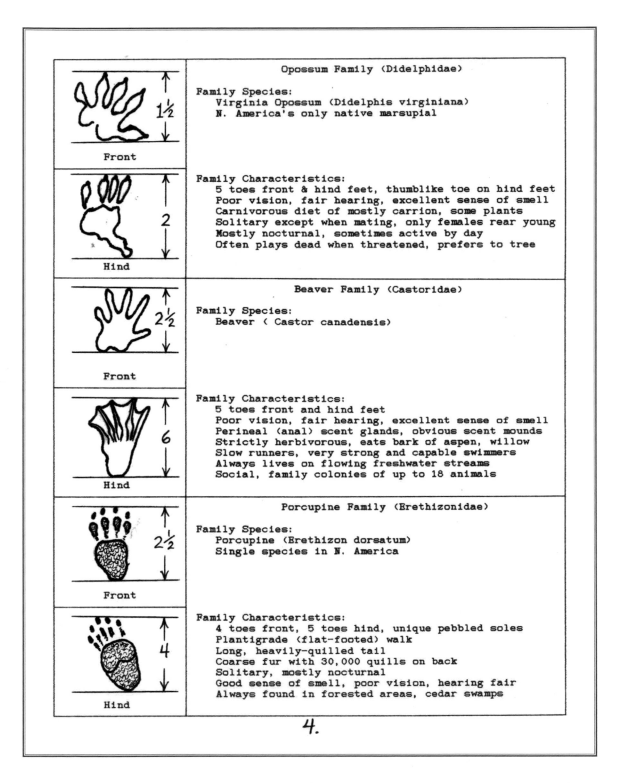

Opossum Family (Didelphidae)

Front — 1½

Hind — 2

Family Species:
    Virginia Opossum (Didelphis virginiana)
    N. America's only native marsupial

Family Characteristics:
    5 toes front & hind feet, thumblike toe on hind feet
    Poor vision, fair hearing, excellent sense of smell
    Carnivorous diet of mostly carrion, some plants
    Solitary except when mating, only females rear young
    Mostly nocturnal, sometimes active by day
    Often plays dead when threatened, prefers to tree

Beaver Family (Castoridae)

Front — 2½

Hind — 6

Family Species:
    Beaver (Castor canadensis)

Family Characteristics:
    5 toes front and hind feet
    Poor vision, fair hearing, excellent sense of smell
    Perineal (anal) scent glands, obvious scent mounds
    Strictly herbivorous, eats bark of aspen, willow
    Slow runners, very strong and capable swimmers
    Always lives on flowing freshwater streams
    Social, family colonies of up to 18 animals

Porcupine Family (Erethizonidae)

Front — 2½

Hind — 4

Family Species:
    Porcupine (Erethizon dorsatum)
    Single species in N. America

Family Characteristics:
    4 toes front, 5 toes hind, unique pebbled soles
    Plantigrade (flat-footed) walk
    Long, heavily-quilled tail
    Coarse fur with 30,000 quills on back
    Solitary, mostly nocturnal
    Good sense of smell, poor vision, hearing fair
    Always found in forested areas, cedar swamps

4.

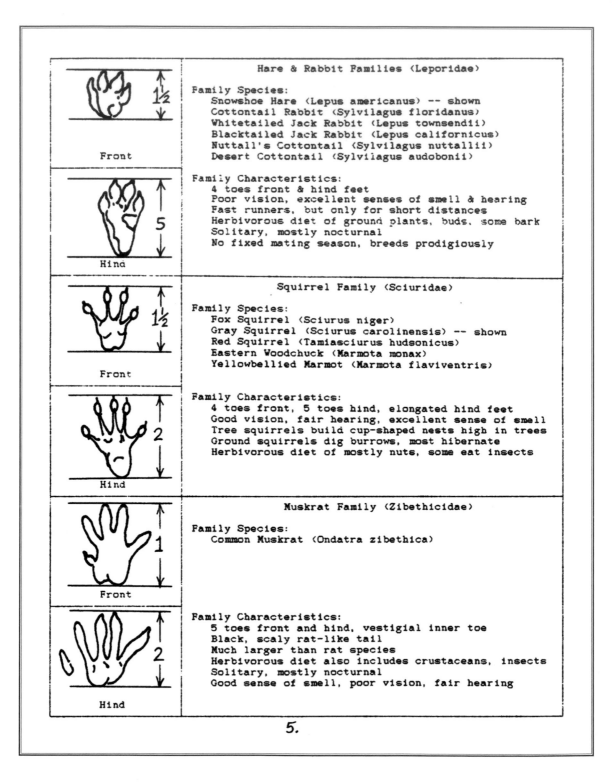

Hare & Rabbit Families (Leporidae)

Front

Hind

Family Species:
Snowshoe Hare (Lepus americanus) -- shown
Cottontail Rabbit (Sylvilagus floridanus)
Whitetailed Jack Rabbit (Lepus townsendii)
Blacktailed Jack Rabbit (Lepus californicus)
Nuttall's Cottontail (Sylvilagus nuttallii)
Desert Cottontail (Sylvilagus audobonii)

Family Characteristics:
4 toes front & hind feet
Poor vision, excellent senses of smell & hearing
Fast runners, but only for short distances
Herbivorous diet of ground plants, buds, some bark
Solitary, mostly nocturnal
No fixed mating season, breeds prodigiously

Squirrel Family (Sciuridae)

Front

Hind

Family Species:
Fox Squirrel (Sciurus niger)
Gray Squirrel (Sciurus carolinensis) -- shown
Red Squirrel (Tamiasciurus hudsonicus)
Eastern Woodchuck (Marmota monax)
Yellowbellied Marmot (Marmota flaviventris)

Family Characteristics:
4 toes front, 5 toes hind, elongated hind feet
Good vision, fair hearing, excellent sense of smell
Tree squirrels build cup-shaped nests high in trees
Ground squirrels dig burrows, most hibernate
Herbivorous diet of mostly nuts, some eat insects

Muskrat Family (Zibethicidae)

Front

Hind

Family Species:
Common Muskrat (Ondatra zibethica)

Family Characteristics:
5 toes front and hind, vestigial inner toe
Black, scaly rat-like tail
Much larger than rat species
Herbivorous diet also includes crustaceans, insects
Solitary, mostly nocturnal
Good sense of smell, poor vision, fair hearing

5.

minimize the time required to go from motionless to top speed. The result is a track that registers more deeply at the toes than at the heels, and trackers should remember that on firmer ground only the toes may imprint. Species that are digitigrade include deer, canids, and cats.

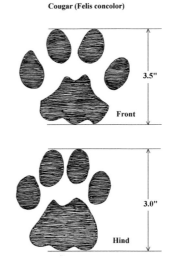

Cougar (Felis concolor)

A drawing of what perfect cougar tracks look like.

Conversely, lack of alertness can get you "caught flat-footed." Plantigrade species walk flat-footed, usually have an elongated hind foot, and are not built for running speed. Inefficient predators, most are omnivorous opportunists, and all have a defensive capability that deters predators. Skunks have a chemical repellent, bears have brute power, porcupines have quills, and *Homo sapiens* mastered fire and weapons.

The way all four footprints are arranged—the "track pattern"—tells how fast an animal was traveling. Differences in the track patterns of walking, trotting, and running animals reveal if an animal was relaxed, on a mission, or in flight. Track patterns for different gaits are nearly universal among four-legged mammals, with track placement for a coyote being similar to that of a whitetail in every gait.

Remember that at a casual walk the hind foot of most animals prints on top of the front track. This learned behavior is generic among animals accustomed to walking uneven terrain. Being able to see its forefeet permits an animal to avoid hazards, and learning to plant the hind feet in the same safe place is a learned habit seen in nearly all species.

At a trot, both hind feet and one forefoot tend to print together in a roughly triangular configuration, with the remaining forefoot printing separately ahead of the others. This ensures that three feet hit the ground almost simultaneously, giving the stability of a tripod, while the remaining forefoot acts as a pivot when those three are brought forward.

At a full run, most quadrupeds adopt a "rocking horse" track pattern in which forefeet are planted together to act as a pivot when the rear feet are brought forward to land on either side of them. When the wide-stanced hind feet make contact, the animal lunges forward, forefeet together and stretched ahead to catch it after a leap that may exceed four times its body length.

Always expect an animal to be in a habitat suitable to its species. In every instance, this will include a nearby watering hole, where wet banks often yield perfect tracks. Suitable habitats must also provide nourishment as well as protection from predators.

Armed with these basics, you're ready to start tracking, whether it's exploring along a backcountry riverbank or determining what animal left prints in your garden at home. To assist, here are tips on tracking some of America's more interesting species.

Cougar or Mountain Lion (*Puma concolor*)

Physical Characteristics: Large cat, weighing from 75 to 250 pounds, with thick black-tipped tail equal to about one-half of body length. Tawny brown coat (pelage) in summer,

One of the most feared animals in the wild, the best method of interacting face-to-face with a mountain lion on a trail is to know as much about the species as possible. (Photo courtesy of Makayla Blevins.)

becoming grayer in winter. Yellow eyes, small rounded ears, lighter upper lip outlined by darker markings.

    Tracks: Large paws, from 3 to 4 inches long, outline rounder than canid tracks, typical of felines. Four toes on each foot, with retractable claws that almost never show in tracks. Tracks will be deepest at the toes, becoming fainter toward the heels.

Habitat: Prefers terrain that affords elevated vantage points, but capable of surviving in almost any habitat.

Diet: Carnivorous, including small deer, rabbits, squirrels, and mice. Eats fresh carrion; like most cats, prefers to kill its own food.

Behavior: Solitary, reclusive, seldom seen. Typically sleeps during daylight, emerging from secluded bedding places to hunt at night.

Relatives: Bobcat, lynx, jaguar, ocelot, housecat.

Gray Wolf (*Canis lupus*)

Physical Characteristics: Largest wild canid, weighing from 60 to more than 135 pounds, with bushy tail that never curls over the back . Pelage varies from black to white to gray, usually with a darker "saddle" on the back. Ears erect, but shorter and less pointed than those of a coyote.

Tracks: Four toes on all feet. Very large paws with claws showing in tracks, from 4 to 4.5 inches long. The two outer lobes of the larger forefeet print most deeply, leaving a chevron-shaped heel print unlike the three-lobed heel prints of coyotes, foxes, and most dogs.

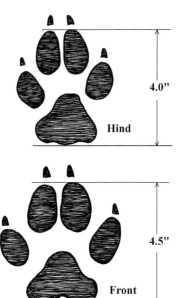

Perfect wolf tracks as they might appear on a soft medium, like snow or mud.

Habitat: Native to the Northern Hemisphere, but now extinct over nearly all of its historical range.

Diet: Primarily carnivorous, but relies heavily on blueberries and car-bohydrate-rich fruits. Uses teamwork to bring down large animals, but pre-fers easy prey. Lone migrating wolves can survive on rodents, insects, and carrion.

Behavior: Strongly social, with packs (families) ranging in size from two to more than a dozen members. All adults care for pups, and pack members bring food to individuals that cannot hunt. Wild wolves do not attack humans, but wolf packs have been known to relinquish their kills to humans.

Relatives: Coyote, fox, dog.

Stealthy, shy pack hunters who cannot distinguish an easily caught sheep or chicken from a deer or grouse, wolves long ago earned the hostility of early settlers whose survival depended on the health of their livestock.

Black Bear (*Ursus americanus*)

Physical Characteristics: Smallest American bear, weighing from 200 to more than 600 pounds (although rare specimens have recorded weights over 900 pounds). Tail short, thickly furred, three to seven inches long. Pelage usually black, occasionally reddish or blue. Ears small and round, muzzle tan or light gray, face and snout more rounded than the brown bear's.

Tracks: Five toes on each foot, all tipped with sharply curved nonretractable claws that show in tracks; elongated hind paws resemble human feet. Although soft-pawed, the bear's sometimes massive weight can leave identifiable impressions in grass and forest humus.

Habitat: Woodlands, with brushy thickets that serve as bedding places. Views human garbage as a food source.

Diet: Omnivorous, the bear's extremely efficient digestive system permits it to subsist entirely on grasses, but a typical diet includes berries, fruits, spiders and insects, fish, nuts, rodents, and carrion. From spring until it dens in autumn, a bear must acquire 25 percent of its mass in body fat.

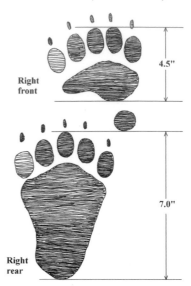

Black Bear (Ursus americanus)

Right front — 4.5"

Right rear — 7.0"

Black bear tracks as they might appear on soft ground; note curved, nonretractable claws for climbing trees.

This trio was actually encountered by the author during an early-summer hike; contrary to dramatic myths, the hikers simply backed away, and there was no indication of hostility from the protective mother.

Behavior: Solitary and reclusive, spending most of the day sleeping in secluded thickets. Prefers to avoid humans, but emboldened by the presence of food.

Relatives: Brown bear, polar bear.

Porcupine (*Erethizon dorsatum*)

Physical Characteristics: Weighs from 8 to 40 pounds. Humped back, short legs. Back and especially tail covered with coarse gray hairs and approximately thirty thousand hollow, barbed quills that are voluntarily detached on contact, but not thrown; no quills on the head or underbelly. Clublike tail, 6 to 12 inches long, used to swat attackers. Rodentlike head, with short muzzle and small round ears. Yellow incisors require constant gnawing to prevent malocclusion.

Tracks: Four toes on forefeet, five toes on hind feet, each tipped with a stout climbing claw. Front track from 2 to 3 inches long, including claws; hind track from 3 to 4 inches long. Plantigrade walk with distinctive pebble-grain soles. Wide, low-slung belly drags in fresh snow, leaving a trough that can obscure tracks. In sand, tracks may be obscured by the heavy tail, which swings back and forth, leaving broomlike striations.

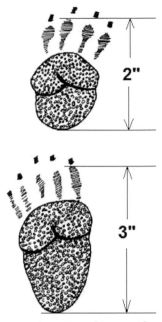

Porcupine tracks as they might appear in soft snow or mud; note pebbled surface of foot soles.

The slow-moving, vegetarian porcupine is entirely nonaggressive, but it is well-armed with thirty thousand very pointed, barbed quills that can make any attacker regret a confrontation; photographers should especially beware the club-like tail.

Habitat: Primarily coniferous forests, but prefers mixed woods with tall deciduous trees that provide secure sleeping places. Every porcupine habitat will include tall trees and a source of fresh water.

Diet: Herbivorous; poplar and other buds in spring, ground plants throughout summer, conifer bark and twigs through winter.

Behavior: Solitary, nearly always nocturnal. Most likely to be seen sleeping high up in a tall tree during daylight hours.

Relatives: The porcupine is the only North American species in its family.

Raccoon (*Procyon lotor*)

Physical Characteristics: Weighs from 12 to more than 45 pounds. Predominantly gray, sometimes reddish, coat. Thickly furred ringed tail. Pointed muzzle, short ears, eyes surrounded by mask of darker fur.

Tracks: Easily identified by long, bulbous tipped toes that permit the raccoon to be a clever manipulator of locks and latches. Best tracking places are shorelines, where mud and wet sand often yield perfect tracks.

Habitat: Woods, thickets, never far from water. A capable climber, habitat always includes tall trees in which to escape enemies.

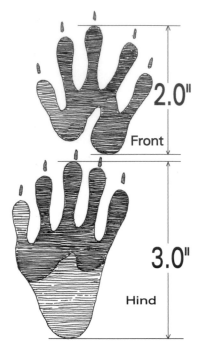

Raccoon tracks as they might appear on soft ground; more darkly shaded areas indicate where the most body weight normally presses downward.

This young adult raccoon exhibits why the species' cuteness often fools hikers into thinking they're tame; raccoons are not friendly, and one that acts unafraid may well be the victim of rabies.

Diet: Omnivorous; frogs, crayfish, insects, fresh carrion, blueberries, and other fruits. Scavenges human garbage, and has notoriety as a chicken thief.

Behavior: Once believed to wash its food (the scientific suffix "lotor" means "washer"), the raccoon has primate-like fingers that enable it to pick out inedible matter.

Relatives: Coati, ringtail.

River Otter (*Lontra canadensis*)

Physical Characteristics: Large aquatic weasel, weighing from 11 to 30 pounds.

Tracks: Five toes on all feet, toes splayed in tracks. Short nonretractable claws register at the end of each toe. Front tracks from 3 to 3.5 inches long, nearly as wide as they are long; hind tracks slightly shorter. Hind toes are elongated and webbed; webbing may show in tracks made in mud, but not on firmer earth.

Habitat: Rivers, ponds, lakes, rarely more than a few yards from the shoreline. River otters can tolerate extremes of cold, but not chemical pollutants, and their presence indicates a body of water is uncontaminated.

Diet: Small fish, crayfish, beaver kits.

Behavior: Normally solitary, but mothers with one to four pups are normal in summer. Avoids humans, but possessed of great curiosity.

Relatives: Mink, wolverine, badger, skunk, sea otter.

River otters are familial, often seemingly playful, and superbly adapted to an aquatic environment, whether it's a lake, river, or beaver pond (where they make beaver young, called kits, regular fare in early summer).

9

WINTER HIKING

Winter in this case means the duration of a season in which air temperatures seldom rise above 32°F in temperate and polar climate zones. Water left outside turns to smooth, slippery ice, the surface of the soil is hard-frozen, and the landscape is usually covered in snow. Precipitation falls in the form of snowflakes, which take different forms mostly according to temperature.

In warm winter temperatures—25°F to 30°F—snow can fall as conglomerated, fluffy lumps; colder times in the 10°F to –5°F range (it seldom snows in subzero temperatures) often result in BB-size balls of white. First snows are fluffy, with nothing under them but earth, and that's when the most snowmen and snowwomen are made. By midwinter in snow-country, where there is never bare ground after a permanent snowfall, layers of falling snow have compacted themselves to an icy hardpack that restricts snowmobiles to groomed trails and roads. Hikers who try to walk through midwinter hardpack might find it impossible. Each step sinks knee deep in a frozen hole that can steal any footwear except a properly tied, ankle-high boot. Upper layers of snow are usually crystalline, solid but crunchy underfoot. But your

Winter hiking in snow country is always an adventure, because just standing around doing nothing can be fatal; a hiker had very much better be prepared under these conditions.

Many unusual sights await the hiker intrepid enough to venture into a frozen winter wilderness, sights that cannot be seen in summer, and species of wildlife that are simply flabbergasted to see a walking human in that environment.

foot doesn't stop there; as you transfer body weight forward to take a step, the next layers give way, and your foot comes to bone-jarring stop after sinking to a depth that reaches perhaps mid-thigh. With each step, you have to pull your foot out of a hole like the one just described.

A wealth of sights, sounds, and experiences await the hiker who has the intrepidity to venture into a frozen forest. Stuff that makes a camera absolutely necessary; you'll probably see things that make others go "Nuh-uh, you're making that up!" Sure, a few species like chipmunks hibernate through the winter (you aren't likely to see a bear, either), but a winter forest is far from dead. A bonus is that the animals that remain active usually leave more obvious tracks and sign, and scat deposits—very important when tracking—are obvious from a distance. Humans are a curiosity in a snow-locked forest; chances are that squirrels, birds, and maybe a deer could actually be drawn to you in an environment where they can be more clearly seen than in any other season.

THE SCIENCE OF LAYERING

The biggest secret to enjoying hiking in snow season is simply not to get cold. No sane person wants to be immersed in iced-over water, but if the hardpack gives way underfoot on a stream bank, you don't want that frigid dunking to become a life-threatening event.

Consider how two lighter blankets retain more body heat under themselves than a blanket that weighs as much as both of them. This is because the all-important layer of dead air trapped between them is loath to give up its warmth. Modern materials help, but the success of the best of them still lies in how much air they trap inside. Dead air is what makes a layered outfit work.

A few outdoor recreationalists, notably snowmobilers and deer hunters, still insist on wearing thick, one-piece jumpsuits that are very warm when they're dry and everything goes according to plan. But if a snowmobile loses a drive belt and its driver has to walk a long distance, or if a deer hunter is forced to negotiate tangled forest to retrieve his trophy, one-piece insulated jumpsuits invariably prove too warm, making them sweat with every exertion. Once wet, even a batting of nonabsorbent synthetic fibers holds sufficient moisture, and evaporates (cools!) just enough to make a jumpsuit feel clammy and cold inside. Very slowly evaporating moisture means a constant loss of body heat.

The advantage of a layered winter outfit over a heavy parka is that it creates more insulation with less bulk and loss of mobility. It's a system, and how efficiently it traps body heat has everything to do with the type of garments worn, the materials, and the sequence in which layers are arranged. Keeping warm isn't rocket science, but it is science; enjoying snow country demands some knowledge of thermodynamics, and layering with today's high efficiency fabrics. Be sure each layer is sized to fit over the layers under it, and every layer fits loose enough to have wrinkles in its fabric. Wrinkles help to trap more dead, motionless air.

A garment's thermal efficiency is determined not by the material, but by the amount of "dead air" trapped within its fibers. Layers of warmed, motionless air are key to retaining body heat. Lighter multiple layers retain heat better than a single, thick layer. A thicker layer of any material will, of course, resist heat loss more than a thinner layer of the same material, but thinner layers enable a wearer to tailor the amount of insulation worn to the amount needed.

Snow does not melt against the outside of a well-insulated garment. If it does, you're losing body heat. The measure of a boot's warmth, for example, is demonstrated by the fact that snow doesn't melt against its outside.

A rise in temperature, slackening of wind, or period of heavy exertion may cause you to perspire, resulting in a need to remove insulation. With a layered

A properly layered outfit enables hikers to tailor the amount of clothing they wear to match exertion levels and temperatures and minimize perspiration.

Exiting a tent on a subzero winter morning illustrates how important a layered outfit can be when it's cold, or at least until you get the fire rekindled and your blood flowing again.

system, you can remove garments as needed to regulate a steady, comfortable body temperature. Discarded garments can be rolled up and stowed in your backpack.

Loose garments are warmer than tight ones. Contemporary fashion dictates dressing in skin-tight clothing. But this is precisely the wrong way to dress in cold weather, because it

In contrast to modern styles, a layered cold weather outfit should comprise loose-fitting garments that trap a maximum of warmed dead air beneath them.

In contrast to modern styles, a layered cold weather outfit should comprise loose-fitting garments that trap a maximum of warmed dead air beneath them.

leaves no dead-air space between skin and clothing. Likewise, avoid the very common mistake of stretching on more pairs of socks, as this will squeeze the feet, inhibiting blood flow, and actually making them colder.

Cotton in any amount or combination is bad. Cotton sucks up and holds moisture, displacing insulating dead air with cooling wetness, and it dries slowly, subjecting its wearer to constant cooling from evaporation. These properties make it an ideal material for towels and wash cloths, but not cold weather clothing.

Cotton only works as the outermost layer. The cotton winter camouflage trousers and jacket worn by military troops and outdoor photographers adds the most warmth when its fabric freezes and minimal air can pass through its threads and a layer of motionless warmed air gets trapped beneath. This works because cotton does absorb water, but the outer layer is so thermally isolated from those below that the moisture becomes ice.

There are essentially three layers in a cold weather outfit: a base layer (long underwear) is first, worn against the skin, followed by an intermediate layer (or two), and finally, a tough, weatherproof outer shell. Each layer performs a specific function that is different from, yet complements, the others, and each component needs to be easily removable to facilitate mixing and matching layers in changing weather conditions.

BASE LAYER: UNDERWEAR

Except for adding garments and layers of insulation to your clothing outfit, there's not a lot of difference between dressing for cold and warm weather hiking. Underwear is one of those differences, and when temps fall to 40°F with rain, or below that temperature without rain, long johns underwear is needed. That means, at least, long underwear pants. I find that long underwear tops are superfluous, because you can design your own warm upper-torso outfit, so long as you abide by the no-cotton rule.

In bygone days, what we now more decorously term a base layer consisted of a one-piece woolen union suit that buttoned up its front and had a button-closed "trapdoor" in its butt for quick trips to the outhouse. Its woolen composition was scratchy against bare, sweaty skin, but being cold was easily the greater discomfort, so for centuries wearers just bore the itchiness. Union suits can still be had, and in a variety of modern materials, as can more contemporary woolen two-piece designs, but coarse wool has become more of a novelty in the comparatively soft lives of today.

Hypothermia can become a problem in any season, almost anywhere in the world. Modern long underwear is woven from polyester fibers. Being essentially made of plastic, the gar-

Perhaps the first real base layer, the union suit kept generations of pioneers and homesteaders warm through their travels.

Base layer pants (sometimes two pairs if it gets really cold) are necessary to winter hiking, backpacking, and camping.

ments absorb minimal moisture compared to cotton, excess water drips from the material, it dries fast from radiated body heat (you can "wear it dry"), and synthetic material remains skin-friendly when wet.

Long john trousers can also be doubled up (usually only in temperatures below 20°F) to more than double the amount of heat retention provided for the legs. As a rule, if your fingers need gloves to keep them warm, your legs need the protection of long underwear pants. If temperatures fall beyond the comfort zone of a single long john trouser, adding another on top of it increases warmth by more than 200 percent by adding another wide layer of warmed dead air, as well as another firewall against the cooling effects of wind.

THE INTERMEDIATE LAYER

Worn over the base layer, an intermediate layer might actually be two or even three layers, depending on activity levels and temperature. Its job is to inhibit loss of body heat from the base layer by providing additional layers of warmed air, while also conducting moisture vapors outward as efficiently as its material allows. Here is where that scratchy wool knit sweater becomes useful, but most folks opt for softer polypropylene "fleece" fabrics.

Knit sweaters have gone out of fashion with today's youth, and that hundred-dollar cable-knit sweater that was a Christmas present from grandma often ends up in a resale shop. I periodically pick up a half-dozen new condition "camping sweaters" for about three dollars each.

PARKA SHELL

For decades I wore an uninsulated or lightly insulated waist-length outer shell jacket, electing to put my own layered insulation below its dense, windproof shield of, preferably, synthetic material, but often GI cotton duck cloth.

One advantage of the GI field jacket, besides its multigenerational heirloom toughness and reliability, has been that it offers plenty of big, bellowed (expandable), glove-friendly pockets with flaps that snap down to secure them. You can literally wear an entire basic survival kit with you that rides so conveniently you might forget that you have some items.

As you gain experience adventuring into places that few people ever visit, seeing sights that go unseen by the most powerful spy satellite, and breathing the cleanest air left on this world, some items will naturally gravitate to selected pockets. This natural evolution is in response to what you learn is most necessary to cope with the environment you're exploring. A desert wanderer might have little use for a fishing kit, just as snowshoes are generally useless in snowless terrain.

Some old-timer winter hikers add sewn-on loops, sometimes just untied loose ends, of cord to the flaps of their pockets, near the snap. The sewn-on cord in either form adorns the pockets, zipper pulls, and even the retaining strap on knife sheaths: anything that you might need to unsnap or open with heavily gloved or mittened hands.

TROUSERS

For the legs, I find that densely woven, wind-resistant nylon six-pocket trousers, like military-type BDUs, worn over base-layer bottoms are equal to most cold weather. In double-digit subzero temps I add a second base-layer bottom, sized large enough to fit over the first. Wool works well here, shielded from the skin by a softer synthetic layer.

One-piece insulated jumpsuits are not recommended, because these don't allow insulation to be added or removed as conditions dictate to maintain a comfortable level of warmth. Insulated coveralls are too warm for even short hikes into the woods, and basically offer the choice of too warm or too cold; they are either on or off. Most hold several pounds of water when saturated, and lower-end models are not rainproof.

SOCKS

Socks can be critical, even lifesaving. Thanks to inadequate footwear and a particularly cold winters, thousands of soldiers throughout history have lost toes, feet, and even their lives to frigid temperatures that proved to be every bit as dangerous as their human enemies. Those who do not lose body parts to cold suffer circulatory and neurological damage, chronic pain, and other unpleasant symptoms that sometimes take years to appear. And once they manifest themselves, various injuries from cold usually last a lifetime. Unless you can fly, protecting your feet from cold is vitally important.

Socks, too, are a system, with a lightweight, slippery, liner sock of nonabsorbent material, covered by a thicker insulated oversock. As mentioned in chapter 1, a two-sock system is recommended year-round. The liner sock is a synthetic fiber (essentially, plastic) material that will not absorb moisture and remains slippery enough to prevent blister-causing friction.

Liner sock manufacturers use words like wicking to sell their products, meaning that synthetic liner socks refuse to absorb moisture and transport perspiration away from the foot. There's no magic in this phenomenon; heat from the foot drives perspiration into the liner, which cannot absorb it, and therefore passes through into the cushioned oversock. From there, moisture passes through a waterproof microfiber bootie (an internal part of most pac boots), and into the usually nonabsorbent boot insulation.

At that point moisture becomes trapped against the boot's shell. Ask any winter camper and they'll tell you that at the end of a day outside, their boots need to be dried. The purpose of a liner sock is to prevent blisters and to make feet feel drier no matter how damp the oversock and boot insulation may become. That alone is enough to keep feet feeling warm and dry(er).

Purpose-made liner socks cost about six dollars a pair at outfitter stores, but department store acrylic dress socks are generally cheaper, and perform nearly as well. Quality oversocks, like the Smartwool brand, retail for about twelve dollars per pair, but most give years of service.

This polyester liner sock/cushioned woolen oversock combo is the most effective sock system to date for keeping feet feel warm and dry.

Once again, this is a clothing application in which cotton in any amount is a bad thing. Cotton socks can make feet feel cold in the warmest boots, and they lose all of their cushion when wet. But a good sock system, like the one described above, helps to get maximum warmth from an inadequate boot. And in any case, it's good to carry spare socks, because even in warm weather, having wet feet for a long time can cause skin problems.

A hiker attempts to dry out cotton socks that have absorbed moisture while hiking.

FOOTWEAR

Proper boots are especially important. If there's snow on the ground you need a full-blown snowpack boot (or pac boot, to use a vernacular so old that it has become this boot design's name). If there's snow on the ground, use only a true pac boot, expressly engineered to keep its wearer warm and comfortable while walking on nothing but snow.

Regardless of claims, a hiking boot with padding, as opposed to actual insulation, is inadequate for winter hiking. Foremost is the fact that a hiking, backpacking, or even mountaineering boot isn't warm enough. To prove that, leave a pair of hiking boots and a set of pac boots outside in freezing temperatures lower than 30°F overnight. Tie-on each pair in the morning, and wear them outside for a two- or three-mile hike; not too far, because your toes will begin to

New back in the day when manufacturers dared to assign comfort levels to pac boots, these LaCrosse −100°F removable-liner models have been facilitating winter activities from fourteen-hour dogsled races to seven-day survival classes, in temperatures as low as −44°F. These old friends, for eighteen years, have always guaranteed warm toes.

freeze in the hikers. Pac boots, by comparison, will warm up when you seat your feet in them. They are so insulated that snow doesn't melt against their outsides, proving that no heat is escaping through their insulation.

A tried-and-true type of pac boot is the removable liner type. Its liner can be taken out and dried, laundered, or exchanged in the field for a dry pair from your backpack. A spare pair of pac boot liners in your pack is always recommended in winter. Not all removable-liner pac boots are the warmest on snow, and comfortable enough to hike in all day, but the warmest and best-fitting pac boots use internal liners.

Another great thing about them, and to a lesser extent, the integral-liner boots described below, is the ideal, padded, and insulated fit from sole to mid-calf, even higher in some designs. No hiking boot has ever matched the ankle and foot protection of a pac boot. Originally made with thin soles,

All else aside, snow doesn't melt against the outer surfaces of boots that are rated for hiking on snow.

with widely spaced tractor treads molded into the usually yellow rubber bottoms (yellow soles were easier to see on people who had fallen in the cold), pac boot soles now come in a variety of thicknesses and with a plethora of tread designs. .

In temps above 0°F, boots with integral liners can be sufficient to maintain comfort all day (temperature ratings are tongue-in-cheek, at best). For temperatures below that, I recommend a full-blown pac boot, with ankle-high uppers, removable liners, and a comfort rating of at least −40°F. Prices for good pac boots (it pays to stick with name brands from manufacturers who have earned a reputation for quality) begin at about eighty dollars.

GLOVES AND MITTENS

Handwear is an imperative, regardless of season, because fingers are even more vulnerable to cold than toes. Mittens are warmer than gloves, but most active outdoorsmen prefer to have fingers operate independently.

All-in-one gloves, lined with high-efficiency insulations like Thinsulate and ComforTemp and encased in weatherproof shells, are usually adequate to 25°F. There exists a wide selection of styles, but my preference thus far is RefrigiWear's warm double insulated cowhide leather work gloves with abrasion pads, priced at about thirty dollars per pair.

In very cold weather, I wear a light, stretch-knit acrylic liner under the main glove. Purpose-made liners are available for around six dollars, but stretch-knit acrylic children's gloves work almost as well, for about one dollar per pair. A big advantage of wearing liners is that the main outer glove can be stripped off to facilitate delicate tasks, like knot-tying, without exposing naked skin. If you think that you'll be wearing liners, be sure that your primary glove is sized large enough.

WINTER HEADWEAR

A warm hat is frequently overlooked, especially by snowmobilers, as they normally wear a helmet. Remove your helmet at a trail stop, however, and you might welcome even a simple

knit watch cap–type cover, available for around three dollars at most department stores.

A hood on your jacket is indispensable, because it guarantees that you'll always have a head covering. Probably best of all are the one-piece, multi-purpose hood/hat/balaclava/mask outfits, made from acrylic, densely woven wind-stopper polar fleece. These are available in a variety of colors, with a base retail price of about ten dollars, and can simply be wadded into a pocket when not in use.

Put all of these together and you have an effective outfit that adjusts to keep you comfortable indefinitely in virtually any weather, from freezing rain and sleet to a subzero blizzard. Our forefathers could only have wished for such immunity to cold when the phrase, "you'll catch your death of pneumonia" had a more ominous tone than it does today.

In most instances, a ballcap and the indispensable hood are the equal of cold.

BEDROLLS

While hiking doesn't imply camping, there exists an almost innumerable list of mishaps that can force a hiker to lay up for a night or two. A fall or misstep can immobilize the toughest person, which reinforces the philosophy of the buddy system; you should never venture alone into places where help might be far away.

A bedroll has proved its value for someone who is in shock from an injury, for someone suffering from hypothermia—for example, falling into a cold river during a freezing rain. Or a person might undergo anaphylaxis (allergic reaction) to a bee sting, blackfly bites, a scorpion sting, or snakebite. Any condition that causes a victim to lose body heat or feel cold is best remedied by a good bedroll.

In days past, a tried-and-true bedroll was a heavy wool blanket, usually a "six-point" (extra-large) that permitted a large man to wrap his entire body. Wool has unmatched insulation properties (natural lanolins, or oils, in the fibers act to repel water), and it retains much of its warmth even in a pouring rain. Speaking from experience, this author has awakened to many a morning covered in snow up to a foot deep, but warm enough inside a wool blanket to not know it.

Down (goose feathers, usually) makes for a lightweight, compressible package, and is still a favorite type of sleeping bag for mountain climbers who never face temperatures above the freezing point of water. Water in its liquid form is the downfall (pun intended) of feather insulation. Down absorbs several times its own weight in moisture, causing the feathers to clump together, and rendering it useless as insulation.

The ideal material at the time of this writing is synthetic fiberfill. Introduced more than four decades ago by the DuPont Corporation as Hollofil, a hair's-breadth hollow plastic fiber, it quickly evolved from there. First was Hollofil 202, with two tunnels running the length of each plastic fiber, then Hollofil 404 with four tunnels, Hollofil 808, and so on.

Making each plastic fiber hollow ensured that it trapped the dead air heated by body warmth. Just as pink fiberglass insulation traps dead air inside house walls to prevent heat from escaping, hollow plastic

Synthetic fiberfill sleeping bags are lightweight, warm, and compact; this one fits in a stuff sack the size of a football.

fibers work to surround a sleeper with their own body heat, encasing them in a cocoon of warmth. The volume of dead air trapped within the fibers is generally referred to as "loft."

By increasing the number of tunnels in each fiber, thereby making each tunnel smaller, their size becomes small enough to exceed the surface tension of a water drop. Put plainly, this means that almost no water can get inside the fibers, so modern synthetic fiberfills absorb water on their outer surfaces and covers only. That phenomenon causes today's sleeping bags to retain 75 percent of their thermal efficiency when wet. It also means that a saturated bag drips almost dry in about fifteen minutes.

But beware down-filled bags. Goose down–filled bags perform very well in temperatures low enough to make water a solid, but get it wet, and a down-filled bag is actually worse than useless. The sodden feathers form wet clumps within their quilted cells, and it will take a week or more under ideal (warm and sunny) conditions to fluff and dry them again.

CANTEENS

Hiking in a winter environment can mean a real change in the way a hiker thinks about many of the items and techniques used. For example, whatever the container in which you elect to transport water, it's a time-proven practice to carry a canteen no more than three-quarters full. Your canteen should slosh as you walk. Like a river, moving liquid doesn't freeze as quickly as motionless liquid, so whenever the ambient temperature falls to the freezing point of water (32°F/0°C), make sure that your canteen's contents have space to move.

Another necessary feature of any wintertime canteen is a wide mouth. Traditional round "pancake" canteens, as well as kidney-shaped GI military canteens, have small mouths to help prevent spillage of what might be life-preserving water. The problem is that in subfreezing weather narrow bottlenecks freeze faster and easier than the liquid contents below. Once the narrow neck of a conventional canteen freezes, it forms an ice plug that can prevent even a drop of water from passing. And because the ice plug conforms to the usually uneven inside contours of a canteen's mouth, it can be impossible to dislodge or thaw in the field.

SNOWSHOES

If you live in or drive through places where winter generally means having snow on the ground from autumn till spring, you should have a functional pair of snowshoes for every hiker,

When powder snow makes you sink up to your hips, you need snowshoes; no one gets far without them.

strapped to every backpack and stowed in every vehicle, even if you live within a hub of civilization. A hard wind can transform four inches of falling snow into four-foot drifts that can trap cars and trucks. Even an Olympic athlete can't wade through hip-deep powder very far without being entirely exhausted and wet from sweat.

And more than a few people have died trying; there have been far too many deaths in recent decades among motorists who found themselves stranded on busy highways during a blizzard. Traffic comes to a halt when the first spin-out blocks the way, and, often dressed in fashionable but weather-inappropriate clothing, motorists have no way of reaching a fuel station whose lighted sign may be clearly visible to them. Snowplows can't get through a highway whose lanes are plugged with stalled, stuck vehicles. Even rescue snowmobiles can't bust deep, soft drifts.

But no snow is too deep for snowshoes. Traditional wood-and-webbing snowshoes have been in use for at least six millennia, and they remained largely unchanged until the late 1990s, when several manufacturers introduced state-of-the-art snowshoes and boot bindings made from the latest high-tech materials. I hung up the ash-and-rawhide military bearpaw snowshoes that I'd been wearing since 1968, strapped on an aluminum-and-Hypalon pair, and never looked back.

The weight of traditional and modern snowshoes is about the same for models rated to carry the same mass, but snowshoes with solid decks of tough fabric have more flotation—the ability to support a load based on surface area and weight distribution—and can offer the same load rating in a smaller snowshoe. One myth is that webbed decking of rawhide or neoprene provides more flotation than tube-frame models with solid decking. Think in terms of two canoe paddles, one with a solid wooden blade, the other with a webbed flow-through blade, like a snowshoe. You don't need to be an engineer to see that the webbed paddle is poorly designed for pushing against water. Per square inch of area inside their frames, solid decks support 27 percent more weight than webbed decks.

Differences in weight between modern and traditional snowshoes are generally attributable to the type of bindings with which each is fitted. Atlas Snowshoe Company claims that a carrying a pound on your feet equates to carrying six pounds on your back, so weight is important; but a few ounces more to have stable, secure, quick-release bindings that won't ice-up is a price I've been willing to pay. As a young trapper, there were many times when I simply sliced through the ice-caked laces of my bearpaws' split-leather bindings with my knife rather than fighting to untie them at the end of an exhausting day. Today you can step into the fastest, most secure, and glove-friendly snowshoe bindings yet conceived and be bound for the back country in a matter of seconds.

The new bindings—which have of late found their way onto several traditional wood-and-webbing snowshoes—almost universally carry stainless steel crampons. In generations past it was often necessary to remove one's snowshoes to climb steep hills, and coming down was an adventure in sliding. Crampons provide traction sufficient to climb any grade your legs can push you up, and are an excellent brake for sure footing on steep descents. And if your path leads across the sun-warmed surface of a frozen lake, the crampons will keep you on your feet in places where you'd otherwise make frequent hard contact with ice.

Northern indigenous tribes know March as the "Moon of the Broken Snowshoes," a time when warming days "rotted" hard-packed snow. Surfaces that had been hard as concrete in February became treacherous with voids hidden below and sun-softened layers that would suddenly cave-in for several feet all around, sending a snowshoer crashing downward into tangled brush. It was common to "bridge" a snowshoe across two solid points when that happened, and with all of a wearer's weight on the unsupported center, wood frames were prone to snap in two. A broken snowshoe could be life-threatening if you've broken trail a mile or two through hip-deep powder that won't support a snowmobile, because you might not be able get back without two snowshoes. Bridging doesn't appear be a problem with the latest generation of aluminum, plastic, or carbon-fiber frames, all of which have proved to be much stronger than wood.

In one innovative instance, frames were exploited to improve snowshoe performance after an engineer at Mountain Safety Research (MSR) mused hungrily about the Christmas cookies his wife was baking while he soaked in hot bath. It struck him that the cookie-cutter principle could be applied to snowshoe frames, and a few months later MSR's Ascent snowshoe was setting new standards for traction. By making the frame a vertical wall of aluminum, the entire snowshoe became a crampon, digging into the most hard-packed snow and enabling wearers to stick to icy hillsides with an almost fly-like ability.

Whichever snowshoe you select, be sure to get one with adequate surface area to support the load you intend to put on them. In the softest powder a large enough snowshoe can only sink three or four inches, and having too much snowshoe is erring on the side of caution. Too small a snowshoe may be worse than no snowshoes, because they might let you sink eight or ten inches into a hole you then have to lift your foot and the attached snowshoe back out of before repeating the process. Generally speaking, the smallest off-trail qualified snowshoe is in the nine-inch-by-thirty-inch range.

Check that the bindings on whichever snowshoe you choose will fit the boots you intend to wear. A common gripe among long-haul dogsled racers who are required to have snowshoes strapped to their sleds is that many snowshoes have "trail" bindings that are too small to the fit full-size pac boots that are needed in subzero temperatures.

Price-wise, both modern and traditional snowshoes cost about the same, starting at around seventy dollars and increasing as features and materials become more sophisticated.

FIRST WINTER CAMP

It was February 1972, and it wasn't by coincidence that I'd elected to make my first attempt at winter camping during a late winter warm spell. I was sixteen, adventurous, and perhaps a little too sure of myself. I'd been knapsacking on multi-night summer excursions since age twelve, but it had been a cold and snowy winter in northern Michigan, and I was hedging my bets. I was vaguely aware that back-packing and camping atop three feet of hardpack snow could be hazardous, but it was an experience I needed to know, so I'd been waiting for a break in the weather to give it a try.

The day I left was warm and sunny, with a high of about 40°F, and meteorologists claimed the warm trend would hold over several days. Water dripped steadily off stalactite icicles that hung precariously from the eaves as I packed my frameless canvas yucca pack, which required careful packing to make sure its load was balanced against unpadded canvas shoulder straps and to ensure that something soft lay between the wearer's back and hard, pointed items.

This hiker, knowing that snowshoeing generates too much body heat to wear his warmer outer garments, has secured his outercoat and gloves under the elastic shock cords of his backpack.

(continued on next page)

THE ULTIMATE GUIDE TO HIKING

I'd already learned the difficult way that wet conditions turned the feather fill of my vintage Korean War GI mummy bag into a sodden clump, so it was either a six-pound, six-point wool blanket or a batting-filled rectangular bag that was equally heavy, but thicker. I opted for the rectangular bag. My tent was a pup-type mountain tent that was held erect by guyed-out poles at either end, and kept taut by a half-dozen stakes arrayed around its perimeter. It was my first real tent, purchased the previous summer after three years of either sleeping under open sky or erecting a shelter everywhere I camped. It had never been exactly waterproof, but it did block wind and give the illusion of shelter.

My leather high-top timberman's boots were treated with bear grease and insulated with thick knit wool socks that could scrub hide right off sweat-softened heels. They slipped around on the melting hardpack, and, despite the grease, were thoroughly soaked when I reached camp, an adventurous six miles from home. I laid a platform of parallel sticks atop the snow and built a fire on it; while the growing blaze melted its way to earth, I kicked snow out of a depression large enough to accommodate my tent, and the guyed-out stakes that kept it standing.

I felt a bit cocky that night as I sat on my backpack in front of a crackling fire. The camp looked good; I was damp, but warm, and it seemed that this winter camping thing wasn't all that tough. People who used to be sixteen might recall how that age is rich in hard knocks, many of which stem from an unmitigated sense of invulnerability. I crawled into my sleeping bag around ten p.m., feeling that I could survive whatever winter threw at me.

I awoke before dawn when a sudden force impacted my body from above. A soft, very cold weight pressed against my cheek, and I began to shiver. I pushed down into the bag and covered my head, trying to make sense of this rude awakening. Around me, I could hear a strong wind that swept through the leafless hardwoods with a ghostly moaning sound. It didn't take much figuring to deduce that my tent had collapsed under heavy snow that wasn't supposed to fall. Whatever the air temperature was, it was below zero, because my nostrils stuck together when I inhaled through my nose, and the loud wind promised that it would feel much colder in the open.

I fumbled in darkness for the nine-volt AM radio that I'd slept with to keep its battery warm. It didn't take long for a depressingly cheerful morning DJ to announce with unwarranted excitement that an unforeseen blizzard had buried northern Michigan under two feet of snow, with an ambient temperature of −20°F and wind chills of −50°F.

I couldn't stay here, that was certain. It was painfully obvious that my sleeping bag was nowhere near warm enough, especially with the tent caved in under a truckload of snow. My leather gloves had been kept unfrozen inside the sleeping bag, but my

(continued on next page)

boots were rock hard. It took real effort to force my feet into those frozen shells, and when I succeeded I was rewarded with toes that ached from cold.

I felt around to find and open the tent's door. From there, I burrowed upward through drifted snow to emerge into a gray, viciously hostile landscape that was almost surreal, and a little nightmarish. The air was thick with driving snow that limited visibility to a few yards, even here in the relative protection of hardwood forest, and the windward side of every tree was white with packed snow.

My cheeks and forehead burned from cold as I kicked snow out of the fire pit that had been blazing just a few hours ago. Not one ember lived now. I pulled a handful of dead bark from a nearby white birch, but my fingers had curled into unfeeling claws, and I couldn't control the strike-anywhere matches well enough to ignite the tinder. One match head flared against my fingertip, burning a blackened hole into the skin, but there was no pain.

Sometimes being stubborn is not a survival trait, and I had crossed the line between toughness and being foolish. I had no effective defense against the blizzard that promised to kill me, and that was a terrifying realization. Boots still unlaced and frozen, I tucked my shotgun under one arm and waded fresh powder snow to a lowland trail that stretched toward home through sheltered cedar swamp. I held my aching ungloved hands under my coat as I hiked, but convulsive shivering made it clear that my body was losing heat from its core.

Activity had made me feel warmer by the time I reached the swamp trail, where lack of wind made it seem warmer yet. I tied my boots, which were now thawed and wet, and that small accomplishment made me think I might live through this. After I'd covered five miles, circulation had returned to my toes, accompanied by excruciating pain, but I'd stopped shivering. My hands didn't feel cold, but the skin over them burned as if they had been scalded. No sight ever looked more attractive than that of my house emerging from whiteout conditions.

Over the next two weeks I watched outer layers of dead skin peel from my fingers, knuckles, toes, and cheekbones, as if those areas had suffered second-degree burns. The damaged skin was red and sore to the touch for several weeks, but eventually healed completely. The recuperative period also gave me time to reflect on what had been done or gone wrong out there, while the pain of healing prompted me to promise myself that such a thing could never happen again. The experience had shaken me with how entirely insignificant a person is to the forces of nature, and I knew well how narrowly I'd escaped gangrene, amputation, and maybe death.

Nor did it escape me that virtually all of my suffering had stemmed from equipment failure, and that spawned a lifelong obsession for functional gear. Today, nearly four decades later, my profession has required spending upwards of a hundred nights per year sleeping on snow, but there has never been a repeat of such misery.

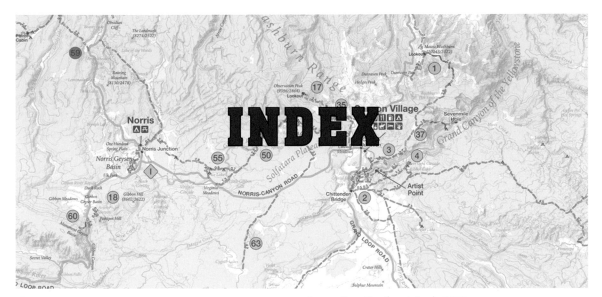

INDEX

paraffin, 50
paraffin-saturated fire wicks, 50
parasites, 73
parka shell, 152
pasta, 90
peccary family *(tayassuidae)*, 134
Pepto-Bismol, for diarrhea, 115
personal locator beacons (PLBs), 126, 127
PLBs. *see* personal locator beacons (PLBs)
"pocket" compass, 11
poison ivy, oak, and sumac, 99–100
polyster liner sock/cushioned woolen
    oversock combo, 153
porcupine *(Erethizon dorsatum)*, 143–144
porcupine family *(brethizonidae)*, 137
Porro prism binocular, 130
precipitation, water from, 72
prismatic compass, 31

Q
Queen Anne's lace *(Daucus carota)*, 94, 95

R
raccoon family *(procyonidae)*, 136
racoon *(Procyon lotor)*, 144–145
radios, 19–20
rattlesnakes, 102, 103
Reader's Digest book *North American Wildlife and Edible Wild Plants* (Perry Medsger), 91
ReadyWise (freeze-dried food), 89
reindeer moss *(Caldonia rangiferina)*, 95–96
"reverse osmosis," 75
rice, 90
river otter *(Lontra canadensis)*, 145
roof prism binocular, 130

S
Schrade's versatile "Extreme" survival knife, 66
scorpions, 104
seepage well, 78–79
self-adhesive moleskin patches, 7

shelf life for stored food, 87
shirts, 11–12
sign, tracking and reading, 133–139
signal fire, 61–62
signaling for help!
    flares, 126–127
    ground-to-air signals, 125–126
    personal locator beacons, 126
    signal mirrors, 125
    signal of threes, 124–125
Signal mirrors, 125
"signal of threes," 124–125
simple pocket or zipper-pull compasses, 31
single-strand fire wick, 51
skunks, 139
Smartwool brand (socks), 153
smoky fire, 47
snakebite, treatment for, 104
snake boots, 103
snakes, 102–104
snow, well-insulated garment and, 149
snowshoes, 158–160
soap bag, 9, 10
socks, 6–7, 150, 152–153
solar condensation still, 77–78
solar still, 77
soles of boots, 4
SOS signal, 124–125
southern black widow *(Latrodectus mactans)*,
    105, 106
spiders
    about, 104–105
    black widow spider *(genus Latrodectus)*,
        105–106
    brown recluse spider *(Loxoscles reclusa)*,
        107
    spiderwebs, 106
spit, to cook small animals, 59
"splint" SAM, for fractures, 113
splitting kindling, 56–57
spoon, camp, 22